THE

PRAYERS

OF THE

BIBLE

DEVOTIONAL

THE

PRAYERS

OF THE

BIBLE

DEVOTIONAL

JOHN HUDSON TINER
ARDYTHE KOLB
SHANNA GREGOR
GLENN HASCALL
VICKIE PHELPS
RACHEL QUILLIN

BARBOUR BOOKS
An Imprint of Barbour Publishing, Inc.

Published by Barbour Books, an imprint of Barbour Publishing, Inc., P.O. Box 719, Uhrichsville, Ohio 44683, www.barbourbooks.com

Our mission is to publish and distribute inspirational products offering exceptional value and biblical encouragement to the masses.

Member of the
Evangelical Christian
Publishers Association

Printed in the United States of America.

If any of you lack wisdom, let him ask of God,
that giveth to all men liberally, and upbraideth not;
and it shall be given him.
JAMES 1:5

Abraham Prays for a Son

*And Abram said, L*ORD *God, what wilt thou give me, seeing I go childless, and the steward of my house is this Eliezer of Damascus? And Abram said, Behold, to me thou hast given no seed: and, lo, one born in my house is mine heir.*

GENESIS 15:2–3

Abram was seventy-five years old when the Lord sent him to Canaan to become the father of a great nation. Abram had no children; yet, ironically, his name meant "exalted father."

About ten years passed. Abram became a successful man, but he had no successor. He asked the Lord, "LORD God, what wilt thou give me, seeing I go childless. . . ?" (Genesis 15:2). The Lord assured him that he would have a son with descendants as numerous as the stars. The next year, his wife was still barren, and she conspired with him to have a child (Ishmael) by her slave woman Hagar.

At age ninety-nine, with Ishmael nearly thirteen years old, Abram must have looked upon the child who had been born through his own efforts as the child of promise. The Lord told him otherwise. He changed Abram's name to Abraham, meaning "father of a multitude," and said that the next year Sarah would have a son.

A year later, Isaac was born. Isaac's name means "laughter." It was a fitting name because Sarah laughed at the idea that a ninety-year-old woman could have a child, and she laughed again in joy when Isaac was born.

Waiting for Isaac gave Abraham time to increase his trust in God. He endured famine, battles, and family squabbles. Abraham grew to become the father through whom nations would be blessed, and also the spiritual father of faith.

Heavenly Father, when we can't see solutions to our human dilemmas, help us remember Your promises to us and wait patiently for You, knowing that nothing is too difficult for You.

Abraham and the Thick and Dreadful Darkness

And he said, Lord God, whereby shall I know that I shall inherit it?
GENESIS 15:8

After Abram arrived in Canaan, raiders captured his nephew Lot and carried away all that he owned. Abram (as he was called then) called three hundred and eighteen trusted fighting men to ride with him to the rescue. Abram freed his nephew and gained back all that Lot had lost.

Despite the victory, Abram felt anxiety. The land was filled with warring tribes and he had but three hundred and eighteen fighting men. The Lord reassured him that he would possess the land (Genesis 15:7). Abram asked a question, not of disbelief, but a practical one about how the land would come into his hands. God did not rebuke Abram for the question. Instead, He directed Abram to seal the promise with an animal sacrifice. Abram cut the animals in half, laid them out, and protected them from birds of prey. At nightfall, Abram was overcome by a thick and dreadful darkness. In a dream, the Lord gave Abram specific information. His descendants would possess a vast land from the Nile River to the Euphrates River—but it would take four hundred years filled with troubles. As for Abram, he would die in peace at a good old age.

Abram went to sleep in darkness but awoke in the light of a promise that the Lord would be with those who have faith in Him.

Lord God, the covenants You make with us are sure and true and can never fail. Praise You for Your faithfulness!

Abraham Prays for His Son Ishmael

Then Abraham fell upon his face, and laughed, and said in his heart,
Shall a child be born unto him that is an hundred years old?
and shall Sarah, that is ninety years old, bear? And Abraham
said unto God, O that Ishmael might live before thee!
GENESIS 17:17–18

Abraham's wife, Sarah, was barren and had not provided her husband a son. In her determination to secure an heir, Sarah offered Hagar, her Egyptian slave, to him. Abraham had Ishmael by the slave woman.

Abraham loved his son and prayed to God, "O that Ishmael might live before thee!" (Genesis 17:18). God explained that His special blessing would go to Abraham's as yet unborn son Isaac. But Ishmael would be blessed, too. God said, "Twelve princes shall he beget, and I will make him a great nation" (verse 20).

Although Abraham had Ishmael circumcised, he was not fully accepted by Sarah. When he was about fourteen years old, Ishmael and his mother were expelled from the camp. After nearly dying in the desert, an angel assured Hagar that Ishmael would not only live but also thrive. Ishmael had twelve sons and a daughter who married Esau, Abraham's grandson.

Ishmael must have continued to have contact with the family. When Abraham died, both Isaac, the son of promise, and Ishmael, the son of a slave, together buried their father.

Children are often put into difficult situations through no fault
of their own. Lord, as Christians, may we accept with
love and respect the treasure of the little ones You give us.

Abraham Prays for Sodom to Be Spared

And Abraham drew near, and said,
Wilt thou also destroy the righteous with the wicked?
Genesis 18:23

Three strangers visited Abraham and announced that the Lord planned to destroy Sodom because of its sin. This disturbing news upset Abraham. His nephew Lot lived in Sodom. Lot's father had died before Abraham, and the rest of the family, including Lot, traveled from Ur of the Chaldees along the Euphrates valley and settled at Haran. Uncle and nephew became close, and Lot followed Abraham to Canaan.

Now Lot lived in Sodom. Two of the three strangers left for Sodom, but one remained behind, and He is identified as the Lord. Abraham asked if Sodom would be spared if fifty righteous people could be found. The Lord agreed. In steps, Abraham reduced the number. Finally, Abraham said, "Oh let not the LORD be angry, and I will speak yet but this once: Peradventure ten shall be found there. And he said, I will not destroy it for ten's sake" (Genesis 18:32). Abraham asked no more, and the Lord left.

Perhaps Abraham reasoned that Lot, his wife, two daughters, and their two fiancés would make six, and surely the city would have four more. But, no. Lot and his family were allowed to escape as the city itself was destroyed.

Although Abraham cared for others, he accepted the fact that God is the final judge of how to deal with sin in His creation.

O Lord, You are both merciful and just. We thank You with
humble gratitude that we can always trust You to do the
right thing in every circumstance of our lives.

Lot Begs to Live in a Little City

Behold now, this city is near to flee unto, and it is a little one:
Oh, let me escape thither, (is it not a little one?) and my soul shall live.
GENESIS 19:20

Lot made some poor choices later in life. Abraham gave Lot the choice of grazing land for his herds in Canaan. Lot decided to leave the Promised Land and go east across the Jordan to an area well watered like Egypt. Another poor choice soon followed: Lot gave up his herdsman's tent to become a city dweller in Sodom. With the city set for destruction, two angels urged Lot to get out quickly with his family. Lot delayed leaving, and the angels took him by the hand and pulled him from the city. As he fled, Sodom was destroyed and his wife died.

The whole valley where Lot had grazed his herds burned like a furnace. He lost his wife, his daughters' husbands, and his wealth. God told him to flee to the mountains, but Lot pleaded to live in a small village. The Lord granted that request. The small city held the same corruption as the larger ones, and Lot eventually moved to the hills to live in a cave.

Lot's preference for a city lifestyle surrounded by evil proved disastrous. Despite this, Peter described him as "righteous" (see 2 Peter 2:7–9). Lot is a figure few Christians would choose to emulate, but he illustrates that God will rescue the righteous despite poor choices.

Thank You, Father, for forgiving us and giving us second chances
when we make foolish decisions. Help us listen to Your Holy
Spirit so that we don't make poor choices in the first place.

Eliezer Prays for a Bride for Isaac

And let it come to pass, that the damsel to whom I shall say, Let down thy pitcher, I pray thee, that I may drink; and she shall say, Drink, and I will give thy camels drink also: let the same be she that thou hast appointed for thy servant Isaac; and thereby shall I know that thou hast shewed kindness unto my master.

GENESIS 24:14

When Abraham was old he gave Eliezer, his trusted servant, the assignment to find a wife for Isaac (Genesis 15:2–3; 24:1–9). But not a Canaanite woman. She should be from Abraham's relatives who lived in faraway Nahor. But Abraham intended to keep Isaac in Canaan to honor God's promise: "Unto thy seed will I give this land" (24:7).

Eliezer loaded ten camels with costly gifts and set out on the long journey. As he neared the spring outside his destination, Eliezer prayed that he would meet a girl who would give him water and water his camels as well. Rebekah, the granddaughter of Nahor, one of Abraham's brothers, did exactly as he had prayed, and watered his camels without being asked (Genesis 24:10–15).

Eliezer gave Rebekah and her family presents and arranged for their immediate return. Rebekah faced a difficult decision. Should she leave with this man she had met only the night before? She made the choice with a three-word reply, "I will go" (Genesis 24:58). The account ends happily because Isaac ran to meet her and "she became his wife; and he loved her" (verse 67).

Abraham faced a difficult situation, Eliezer was in stressful circumstances, and Rebekah had a hard choice to make. All three put their faith in God to lead them, and He gave them a good outcome.

Heavenly Father, Abraham, Eliezer, and Rebekah were all obedient to You and took first steps by faith in their difficult situations. Help us follow their examples and step out in faith when we face challenges.

Jacob Prays for Protection

And Jacob vowed a vow, saying, If God will be with me,
and will keep me in this way that I go, and will give me bread to eat,
and raiment to put on, so that I come again to my father's
house in peace; then shall the LORD be my God.
GENESIS 28:20–21

Rebekah and Isaac had twin sons: Esau the firstborn and Jacob, born holding Esau's heel. Esau was a far-ranging hunter, but Jacob stayed at home. One day when Esau returned from an exhausting hunt, he asked his younger brother for some stew. Isaac proposed selling it to him for his birthright—his inheritance—and Esau accepted the offer.

Years later, when Isaac was old and blind, he asked Esau to hunt wild game for a tasty meal. While Esau was away on the hunt, Jacob, with the help of his mother, conspired to deceive Isaac and receive his brother's blessing. Esau, devastated at the loss of his father's blessing, seethed with anger.

Jacob escaped Esau's wrath by traveling to his mother's family in search of a non-Canaanite wife. The trip would put him far away from his brother and give Esau time to cool down. Jacob realized his desperate situation and prayed for God to watch over him during the journey. He prayed for himself, asking God for food to eat, clothes to wear, and a safe return home (Genesis 28:20–21).

Jacob left behind an angry brother and a confused and weary father. His mother died during his absence—he never saw her again. The crafty Jacob could not restore a broken family with a selfish prayer. Repentance, not regret, would be required.

Father, thank You for putting us in families. May we learn
to love one another and show grace to one
another despite our differences.

Jacob Prays for Safety

Deliver me, I pray thee, from the hand of my brother,
from the hand of Esau: for I fear him.
GENESIS 32:11

Because he feared the threats of Esau after tricking him out of his father's blessing, Jacob escaped to his uncle Laban, whom he served by tending flocks for twenty years, including seven years each for the privilege of marrying Laban's daughters, Leah and Rachel. During those twenty years, Jacob gained great wealth and eleven sons. (Benjamin would be born on his return to Canaan.) Jacob decided to go home with his wives, children, and flocks to face what he feared would be the dangerous wrath of his brother.

As Jacob neared Canaan, he received word that Esau was coming with four hundred fighting men. Jacob was concerned for the safety of the mothers and their children, especially Rachel and her only son, Joseph.

His prayer before that fateful meeting with Esau has become a model prayer. First, he honored God, and then he admitted that he was unworthy. Next, he made a specific request: "Deliver me, I pray thee, from the hand of my brother, from the hand of Esau." He frankly admitted that he was afraid. Finally, he put his trust in the Lord, recalling God's promise to make his descendants like the sand of the sea (see Genesis 32:9–12).

The reunion of Esau and Jacob is one of the most emotional scenes in the Bible. Esau ran to Jacob and embraced him, and they cried. When shown Jacob's peace offering, Esau declined it, saying, "I have enough, my brother" (Genesis 33:9).

Jacob confronted a crisis with prayer and humility.

Father, when we face fearful situations, may we always put
our trust in You, knowing that You have our best interests
in mind and will work out the details as we obey You.

Moses Questions God

*And Moses said unto God, Who am I, that I should go unto Pharaoh,
and that I should bring forth the children of Israel out of Egypt?*
Exodus 3:11

Moses followed a roundabout path before the Lord spoke to him from the burning bush: born to a slave family but raised in Pharaoh's palace, he escaped from Egypt after killing a slave driver, then married a women of Midian and tended sheep for forty years.

Now he stood before the Lord at the burning bush and learned his destiny. God explained that He had heard the cry of His people in Egypt and intended to rescue them. Moses must have rejoiced at that news. Then God told him, "I will send thee unto Pharaoh, that thou mayest bring forth my people the children of Israel out of Egypt" (Exodus 3:10). His heart must have fallen when he learned he would be doing the leading. Moses objected to God's plan. He had been away from his people for most of his eighty years. He had not even circumcised his own son.

Moses raised question after question in an attempt to avoid his assignment: *Who am I to do this? Who should I tell them You are? What if they don't believe me?* But God answered each of his questions: "I Am That I Am: and he said, Thus shalt thou say unto the children of Israel, I Am hath sent me unto you. And God said moreover unto Moses, Thus shalt thou say unto the children of Israel, the Lord God of your fathers, the God of Abraham, the God of Isaac, and the God of Jacob, hath sent me unto you" (verses 14–15).

Moses learned, as we also recognize, that the Lord strengthens and prepares us for whatever task He has for us.

*Thank You, heavenly Father, that whenever You call us to a
task You promise to equip us. Our competence comes from You.
Therefore we can do all things through Christ who gives us strength.*

Moses Asks God to Send Someone Else

*And Moses said unto the LORD, O my LORD, I am not eloquent, neither
heretofore, nor since thou hast spoken unto thy servant: but I am slow
of speech, and of a slow tongue. . . . O my LORD, send, I pray thee,
by the hand of him whom thou wilt send.*

EXODUS 4:10, 13

At the burning bush, Moses continued to raise objections as he
listened to God's plans for him. Moses asked what to do if the
elders of Israel did not listen to him. The Lord gave him two quick
demonstrations. He turned Moses' staff into a snake and back
again. Moses plunged his hand into his cloak, and it came away
leprous. When Moses returned his hand to the cloak, God restored
his hand. Moses tried yet again. He said he was not an eloquent
speaker. God dismissed that objection. Before appearing to Moses,
He had called Aaron from Egypt to rendezvous with Moses and be
the spokesman during the confrontation with Pharaoh.

Moses had now run out of excuses. He came to the heart of the
matter—Moses was reluctant to accept his destiny. He said, "Send,
I pray thee, by the hand of him whom thou wilt send" (Exodus
4:13). But God had prepared Moses for the job given him. Moses
had been born a Hebrew but was raised as a prince of Egypt, and
he later learned to shepherd wayward flocks.

Was Moses afraid to go back to Egypt? Or had he found a
comfortable life he didn't want to leave with a wife and children in
Midian? His concerns mirror many of our own fears and aversions
to tasks for which God has prepared us. We cannot censure Moses
without recognizing the same faults in our own natures.

*Father, forgive us when we stall and make excuses for not doing the
tasks You call us to do. Help us get our priorities straight by
seeking first the kingdom of God, knowing that You
will then supply us with everything we need.*

Moses Complains That No One Listens to Him

And Moses spake before the LORD, saying, Behold, the children of Israel have not hearkened unto me; how then shall Pharaoh hear me, who am of uncircumcised lips?
EXODUS 6:12

When Moses returned to Egypt, the Israelites did not rally behind him. They would not listen because of their discouragement and harsh labor. They complained, "Ye have made our saviour to be abhorred in the eyes of Pharaoh" (Exodus 5:21). When directed to go to Pharaoh, Moses asked the Lord, "The children of Israel have not hearkened unto me; how then shall Pharaoh hear me?" (Exodus 6:12).

Pharaoh ruled a great and prosperous country that wielded enormous influence in the region. For centuries it had survived disasters that overwhelmed other countries. Abraham and Joseph's families had both traveled to Egypt for help during times of famine.

Moses' message to Pharaoh was simple: "Let my people go" (Exodus 7:16). Pharaoh refused to listen to Moses. The first plague turned the waters of the Nile into blood. Fish died. The people could not drink the water. But nine more plagues were required before Pharaoh relented. He told the Israelites to leave and take their flocks and herds with them. Later he changed his mind and came after them.

Despite Moses' complaints, questions, lack of progress, and his statements falling on deaf ears—both those of Pharaoh and those of his own people—Moses pressed ahead with the Lord's work. We can see in him the value of doing our part and relying on God to do the rest.

We thank You, gracious Father, that even when others won't listen to us, we can speak to You 24/7 and know that You will hear and respond to us. May we discipline ourselves to listen to others as well.

Moses: "They Are Almost Ready to Stone Me"

And Moses cried unto the LORD, saying,
What shall I do unto this people? they be almost ready to stone me.
EXODUS 17:4

When Moses led the Israelites out of Egypt, he may have believed that compelling Pharaoh to free them was the hard part. He would discover otherwise, because each new hardship launched them into a furious outburst against him and against God.

When the Israelites huddled in fear against a body of water as Pharaoh's army advanced, God parted the waters for their escape. The enemy army disappeared under the returning waves. After days of travel in the desert, they forgot what God had done for them. They complained of thirst. God provided sweet water and next had the Israelites camp by springs and palm trees. No longer thirsty, they claimed that in Egypt they were well fed. God gave them quails for meat and manna for bread.

Seventy-five days into their escape, they trekked through a dry desert. At Horeb they asked why Moses had brought them out of Egypt to die of thirst. Moses asked God, "What shall I do unto this people? they be almost ready to stone me" (see Exodus 17:4). At God's direction, Moses struck a rock to release a stream of fresh water.

In every case, God provided for the needs of His people. He continues to do so today. Let us be mindful and thankful for His rich blessings that fall upon us each day.

Jehovah Jireh, our Provider, how soon we forget what marvelous things You have done for us. Please forgive us for our dullness and lack of gratitude, and open our eyes to see the wondrous deeds You do on our behalf.

Moses Asks God to Spare His People

And Moses besought the L<small>ORD</small> his God, and said, L<small>ORD</small>, why doth thy wrath wax hot against thy people, which thou hast brought forth out of the land of Egypt with great power, and with a mighty hand?
E<small>XODUS</small> 32:11

Moses and the Israelites had traveled for three months in the desert when they came to Mount Sinai. God called Moses to the mountain to receive the Ten Commandments and other laws of the covenant. God specifically said, "Ye shall not make with me gods of silver, neither shall ye make unto you gods of gold" (Exodus 20:23). But the Israelites had made a golden calf to worship during the forty days that God spoke to Moses on the mountain.

While still on the mountain, God told Moses that the people had become corrupt. He described them as a stiff-necked people and threatened to destroy them. Moses described them as "your people" rather than "my people." God said He would make Moses a great nation.

Although he did not defend the people, Moses did not hesitate to plead for mercy based on the strength of God. He insisted they were God's people—the ones He had brought out of Egypt. God had promised that the world would be blessed through Abraham. Moses did not want to be a new "Abraham" and build a new great nation. His plea honored God rather than diminishing the sin of Israel, and God relented.

Moses' appeal to God shows that a strong prayer is one that recognizes God's power and mercy.

We give thanks to You, Lord, for You are good and Your mercy endures forever. May we never fail to tell the world that You alone are the one true God.

Moses Asks God to Forgive
Israel's Great Sin

*And Moses returned unto the Lord, and said, Oh, this people have
sinned a great sin, and have made them gods of gold. Yet now,
if thou wilt forgive their sin—; and if not, blot me, I pray
thee, out of thy book which thou hast written.*

Exodus 32:31–32

While on Mount Sinai, the Lord told Moses that the Israelites had
become corrupt. But He did not describe the extent of their great
sin. Moses came down from the mountain and saw the revelry of
the people as they worshipped the golden calf. While in Egypt
Pharaoh had asked, "Who is the Lord, that I should obey his voice
to let Israel go?" (Exodus 5:2). Now the Israelites, by their actions
in worshipping the golden calf, asked a similar question.

Moses tossed the calf in the fire, ground it to powder, scattered
it in the water, and made the Israelites drink it. He called the
Levites to take up swords. They rushed through the camp and
killed three thousand.

Moses prayed for forgiveness: "If thou wilt forgive their sin—;
and if not, blot me, I pray thee, out of thy book which thou hast
written" (Exodus 32:32). Moses, like God, had a heart of love and
compassion. He offered himself as a sacrifice. God would have
none of it. God had a greater sacrifice for sin—His own Son.

For forty days, the people had been without clear guidance
while Moses was on the mountain. Their impatience and rebellious
behavior began a cycle of idolatry that persisted for centuries.
Christians are rewarded when they develop the ability to serenely
accept any delay of God's plans for them.

*Longsuffering Father, how patient You are with Your rebellious
children. Thank You for sending Jesus to bear the punishment that we
deserved and for gently drawing us to You by Your Holy Spirit.*

Moses Asks for God's Presence

*Now therefore, I pray thee, if I have found grace in thy sight,
shew me now thy way, that I may know thee, that I may find grace
in thy sight: and consider that this nation is thy people. . . .
If thy presence go not with me, carry us not up hence.*

EXODUS 33:13, 15

Moses, in the verse quoted above, asked God to be with His people. Instead, God said an angel would go with them. Moses, however, believed other nations should see their special relationship with the Lord. Other people believed in false gods with limited kingdoms. They thought that some false gods ruled the forests, others lived on hilltops, and some ensured good hunting while others brought abundant harvests. Moses and the Israelites had but one God who was not limited by geography and who supplied all of their needs.

Moses persisted in his request that God accompany His people. Once again God relented: "I will do this thing also that thou hast spoken" (Exodus 33:17). The Tabernacle, a tentlike structure, described by God earlier, would be a visible sign of His presence.

The Israelites, who had given up their gold to make an idol, now gave up their ornaments and much more to fashion a complex portable place of worship filled with the glory of God. It specifically showed to the surrounding nations that God was with them. The tabernacle contained the ark of the covenant and the stone tablets engraved with the Ten Commandments.

Christians today pray for God's presence because, like Moses, they know that without Him, wealth like that of a land flowing with milk and honey is a meaningless prize.

*Holy Father, how privileged we are to be Your children and to
experience Your constant presence in our lives. We thank You
for Your promise never to leave us nor forsake us.*

Moses Asks to See the Glory of God

I beseech thee, shew me thy glory.
Exodus 33:18

After ensuring the presence of the Lord with His people during their dangerous travels, Moses turned to a request of a personal nature. He asked to see the glory of God. Glory is the biblical figure of speech for God's presence. Other Old Testament prophets heard from God in dreams and visions. Moses, on the other hand, had been in the presence of God. He was asking for even more—to see the very face of God.

We recognize a person most easily by a close view of the person's face. His face can also reveal his character, whether subservient or commanding. A person with a commanding presence can cause one who is approaching to stop short. The absolute power of God would overwhelm Moses. God said, "Thou canst not see my face: for there shall no man see me, and live" (Exodus 33:20).

God did not entirely dismiss Moses' request. Instead, Moses stood in the shelter of a gap in a rock and God protected him by His hands as He passed.

Moses' request was an expression of what Christians feel as they grow closer to the Lord. They develop an earnest desire to experience God more deeply and fully. They see more of His glory as they learn His Word and experience His goodness.

Restore us, Lord God Almighty;
make Your face shine on us, that we may be saved!

Aaron Asks for a Priestly Blessing

*The Lord bless thee, and keep thee: the Lord make his face
shine upon thee, and be gracious unto thee: the Lord lift
up his countenance upon thee, and give thee peace.*
Numbers 6:24–26

Aaron, the older brother of Moses, was called into service to speak for Moses. He teamed up with Moses as both a leader and a messenger for forty years. The position put him in danger with Pharaoh in Egypt and in intense pressure from his own people. Although he survived the dangerous meetings with Pharaoh, he could not withstand the pressure from his own people. He created a golden calf idol for the Israelites when Moses stayed long on Mount Sinai receiving God's Ten Commandments.

Aaron, like Moses, did not enter the Promised Land. He died at age 123 on Mount Hor. However, before he died and after the law was given, Aaron and his sons became the priests of Israel. For centuries the prayer that God gave Aaron reminded Israel that they were blessed. Today, in many churches, the prayer is used as a basis for the benediction, the dismissal prayer, with the phrase "May the Lord bless you" reminding Christians of God's love for them.

Blessings are a powerful expression of love. Jesus, in his Sermon on the Mount, pronounced nine blessings, beginning with "Blessed are the poor in spirit" (Matthew 5:3). The heavenly Father's rich blessings come down on everyone who puts their faith in Him.

Praise God from whom all blessings flow!

Moses Asks for Daily Blessing

And it came to pass, when the ark set forward, that Moses said,
Rise up, LORD, and let thine enemies be scattered; and let them
that hate thee flee before thee. And when it rested, he said,
Return, O LORD, unto the many thousands of Israel.
NUMBERS 10:35–36

After camping at the foot of Mount Sinai for almost two years, the cloud lifted from the tabernacle. It signaled the Israelites to begin their trek to the Promised Land. They set out at the command of the Lord through Moses. He put the ark of the covenant at the front of the procession, and the cloud led them as they set out each morning.

Moses began each day with the same prayer: "Rise up, LORD, and let thine enemies be scattered; and let them that hate thee flee before thee" (Numbers 10:35). The Lord provided His protection when the Israelites walked with Him, but with distressing frequency they would complain and be faithless by marrying foreign women and bowing to false gods. Despite their grumbling and sinful actions, the Lord guided the Israelites to the Jordan River with the Promised Land in sight. But because of fear and lack of trust in Him, the generation that marched from Mount Sinai perished in the wilderness.

Moses' daily prayer gives us an example to begin each day's journey with prayer, asking for God's blessings and protection. Once we put ourselves in God's hands, it is our responsibility to trust in Him and move forward without fear. Our safety and that of our family is not in our strength but in the favor of God.

Almighty God, You are our great defender,
and we choose to put our trust in You today and every day.

Moses Prays for Help

*I am not able to bear all this people alone, because it is
too heavy for me. And if thou deal thus with me, kill me,
I pray thee, out of hand, if I have found favour in thy
sight; and let me not see my wretchedness.*

NUMBERS 11:14–15

For all his positive leadership qualities, Moses struggled with
delegating, a fact that both the Lord and his father-in-law, Jethro,
recognized. Jethro noticed that Moses tried to mediate all of the
disputes within the camp, from petty arguments to major problems.
The lines of petitioners grew long as Moses sat as judge and
struggled to mediate the disputes.

Jethro cautioned, "Thou wilt surely wear away. . . . Thou shalt
provide out of all the people able men, such as fear God, men of
truth, hating covetousness; and place such over them. . .and let
them judge the people at all seasons: and it shall be, that every great
matter they shall bring unto thee" (Exodus 18:18, 21–22). Moses
followed Jethro's wise advice. (Read Exodus 18:13–27.)

Later, as the laws for proper conduct under the covenant with God
were laid out in writing, the trials of leadership once again became too
great. Moses complained, "I am not able to bear all this people alone,
because it is too heavy for me" (Numbers 11:14). The Lord told Moses
to select seventy of Israel's leaders. The Lord filled them with the same
spirit as Moses, which they confirmed by prophesying. Moses no
longer had to carry the weight of leadership alone.

Sometimes God gives us a mission, but He also surrounds us
with others who can act for us. If we first put our trust in the Lord
and pray for guidance, He will show us how to put our trust in others.

*Father, You have made Your Church to be members of one body and have
equipped each part with specific gifts. Help us know when to serve
with our gift and when it is someone else's place to serve.*

Moses Asks How to Feed the People

*And Moses said, The people, among whom I am, are six hundred
thousand footmen; and thou hast said, I will give them flesh,
that they may eat a whole month. Shall the flocks and the herds
be slain for them, to suffice them? or shall all the fish of the
sea be gathered together for them, to suffice them?*
Numbers 11:21–22

As the Israelites trudged through the wilderness, God provided
manna for them to eat. But they complained, "We never see
anything but this manna." They kept thinking about the food
they had in Egypt. "Why did we ever leave Egypt?" they asked.
Apparently they had forgotten how hard they worked for their
Egyptian meals. God first provided manna when they were in a
difficult situation in the wilderness. The necessities alone no longer
satisfied them.

Moses cried to the Lord, "Whence should I have flesh to give
unto all this people? for they weep unto me, saying, Give us flesh,
that we may eat. . . . And the Lord said unto Moses, Is the Lord's
hand waxed short? (Numbers 11:13, 23). He demonstrated His
power by sending a wind that drove great flocks of quail from the
sea. The Bible says the people collected far more of the birds than
they needed.

The Israelites did not recognize God as their provider. They
were hungry, but not for the Word of God. Jesus taught believers
to pray: "Give us this day our daily bread" (Matthew 6:11), and
Paul wrote, "Having food and raiment let us be therewith content"
(1 Timothy 6:8). Giving thanks for a meal reminds us that the
Lord not only provides food but all else that we need.

*Gracious Father, You have promised to provide for all our needs
according to Your riches in glory by Christ Jesus. May we always
remember to show our gratitude for Your faithfulness.*

Moses Prays for His Sister's Healing

And Moses cried unto the Lord, saying,
Heal her now, O God, I beseech thee.
Numbers 12:13

Moses had a brother and a sister. Miriam, the oldest, had watched over him as he floated in the reed basket on the Nile. Aaron was three years older than Moses, as we learn in Exodus 7:7. Moses, then, was the baby brother to both Miriam and Aaron. However, God chose Moses to lead them and all the Israelites to the Promised Land.

While in the wilderness, Miriam and Aaron criticized Moses for marrying a Cushite woman.

In this incident, scripture lists Miriam first as condemning Moses. Elsewhere Aaron is always listed first. Either she spoke first or took the lead in some other way. God turned her skin as white as snow with leprosy for her disapproval of Moses. Aaron's anguish at seeing his sister with leprosy immediately caused him to cry to Moses, "Alas, my lord, I beseech thee, lay not the sin upon us, wherein we have done foolishly, and wherein we have sinned" (Numbers 12:11).

Moses' prayer was heartfelt and instant: "Heal her now, O God, I beseech thee" (verse 13). Miriam lived outside the camp for seven days and returned fully healed.

Moses spoke without hesitation. He didn't linger over the wrong she had done. He forgave her instantly. Love of family overcomes wrongs, and in the family of Christians, a fully forgiving heart is one we can all work toward achieving.

Father, You have taught us that love covers a multitude of sins.
Help us treat our loved ones in the way that we would like to be
treated—with an abundance of grace, love, and forgiveness.

Moses: Forgive the People

Pardon, I beseech thee, the iniquity of this people according unto the greatness of thy mercy, and as thou hast forgiven this people, from Egypt even until now.
NUMBERS 14:19

Before entering Canaan, Moses sent twelve spies to discover the lay of the land. The spies found a rich country, but the cities were secured with walls. Two of the spies, Joshua and Caleb, counseled that with God's help they could take the land. The other spies feared the inhabitants. "We were in our own sight as grasshoppers, and so we were in their sight. . . . Were it not better for us to return into Egypt?" (Numbers 13:33; 14:3). Joshua pleaded with the people to take courage. Instead, they took up stones to kill him.

Moses prayed to God, "Pardon, I beseech thee, the iniquity of this people according unto the greatness of thy mercy, and as thou hast forgiven this people, from Egypt even until now" (Numbers 14:19). The Lord replied that he would forgive them. But those who agreed with the ten spies would not enter the land. He told the people, "Your carcases shall fall in this wilderness; and all that were numbered of you, according to your whole number, from twenty years old and upward which have murmured against me" (verse 29). They would be exiled to the wilderness for forty years. Only Joshua and Caleb would survive to enter the Promised Land.

The Israelites trembled in the face of the "giants." Today we have their reaction to the bad report to encourage us not to be daunted by adversary but to instead choose faith over fear.

Holy Father, when troubles loom before us, remind us to compare the size of the "giants" not with ourselves but with You. You, mighty God, are far bigger than any "giant" that would try to keep us from receiving what You have promised.

Israel Asks for Relief from the Snakes

Therefore the people came to Moses, and said, We have sinned,
for we have spoken against the LORD, and against thee;
pray unto the LORD, that he take away the serpents
from us. And Moses prayed for the people.
NUMBERS 21:7

Time and again in the wilderness the people complained against
Moses and God. "There is no bread, neither is there any water; and
our soul loatheth this light bread" (Numbers 21:5). The Israelites
numbered at least six hundred thousand and probably many more.
Yet what God provided kept all of them alive and healthy in the
wilderness.

As punishment for their complaining, God caused the camp to
come alive with snakes whose venom killed many of the Israelites.
Usually the Bible records how Moses took it upon himself to
go before the Lord in prayer for the people. In this instance, the
Israelites recognized their sin and asked Moses to intercede for
them with God. At God's direction, Moses made a bronze snake
and put it on a pole. When the people dying of the poisonous
venom looked at the snake, they lived. Looking toward the metal
snake showed they recognized their sin.

In one of the most surprising passages of the New Testament,
Jesus identified Himself with the serpent. He used the imagery to
reveal to Nicodemus how He would die for mankind's sin.

The snake incident is the last recorded rebellion of the people
in the wilderness. They learned—as we should—that life is more
richly lived in obedience than in rebellion.

Jesus, You said that if You would be lifted up from the earth,
You would draw all people to Yourself. Thank You for allowing
Your tortured and torn body to be lifted up on the cross
so that we can look to You for our salvation.

Moses Prays for a Leader

And Moses spake unto the LORD, saying, Let the LORD,
the God of the spirits of all flesh, set a man over the congregation.
NUMBERS 27:15–16

At age 120 years, Moses arrived at the Jordan River. The Israelites prepared for the second time to enter the Promised Land. The Lord informed Moses that he would see the land but not enter it. Moses, thinking not of himself but of the people, prayed for an effective leader to take his place "that the congregation of the LORD be not as sheep which have no shepherd" (Numbers 27:17). Moses was to lay his hands on the new leader, Joshua, in the presence of the priest and all the people. In selecting Joshua, God said He wanted someone who "at his word shall they go out, and at his word they shall come in" (verse 21). This imagery is of a shepherd.

Comparing a leader to a shepherd is found throughout the Bible. Jesus said, "I am the good shepherd: the good shepherd giveth his life for the sheep" (John 10:11). Unlike other herdsmen who walk behind livestock and drive them, a shepherd walks in front of and leads the sheep. When danger threatens, the shepherd faces the threat first.

Moses' concern was for the next generation. Like Moses, good Christian leaders invest in training and identifying those who can lead the younger generation in the path of righteousness.

> *Thank You, Father, for the shepherds to whom You have*
> *entrusted our care. They keep watch over us as those who*
> *must give an account. May we submit to them in a way*
> *that will make their work a joy and not a burden.*

Moses Blesses the Tribes

The eternal God is thy refuge,
and underneath are the everlasting arms.
DEUTERONOMY 33:27

Moses' life was drawing to a close. Those of his generation who left Egypt had died. Miriam, his sister, died in the desert and was buried at Kadesh, where Moses had sinned by referring to himself and Aaron as the ones who brought forth water from the rock and failed to give God credit. His brother Aaron had died at age 123 on Mount Hor. Moses now saw the Promised Land from Mount Nebo. At age 120, he had lived a full and interesting life—forty years in the household of Pharaoh, forty years as a shepherd in Midian, and forty years as a shepherd of the people in the wilderness.

We read in Deuteronomy 33 Moses' final address to the people. His speech was a prayer of blessing for each of the tribes. He began by describing the power and lovingkindness of God. Moses then prayed for the tribes of Israel, identifying them by name and describing something specific and positive about each one. Moses was from the tribe of Judah. He said that tribe would defend God's cause. Levi would watch over God's Word and guard His covenant. He went through a roll call of the sons of Israel with his prayer.

The content of Moses' prayer—praises for God and prayers for others with specific, positive language—is an example that Christians can use in their daily talks with God.

Abba Father, how grateful we are that we can come before Your throne with clean hands and confidence because of Jesus' death on the cross. We don't have to perform any rituals or use fancy words; we just have to humble ourselves as Your children.

Joshua Complains

*And Joshua said, Alas, O LORD God, wherefore hast thou at all
brought this people over Jordan, to deliver us into the hand of the
Amorites, to destroy us? would to God we had been content,
and dwelt on the other side Jordan!*

JOSHUA 7:7

Joshua had served as Moses' aide since his youth (see Numbers
11:28). He, along with Caleb, entered Canaan as a spy and urged
his fellow Israelites to occupy the land. Forty years passed before
they did so, with Joshua as commander in chief, following the death
of Moses. After crossing the Jordan, Joshua met his first resistance
at the walled city of Jericho. His army took the city in seven days
by following God's battle plan.

At their next city, Ai, Joshua's soldiers fled in an ignoble defeat.
Joshua cried out to the Lord at the stunning setback. "What shall
I say, when Israel turneth their backs before their enemies! For the
Canaanites. . .shall hear of it, and shall environ us round, and cut
off our name from the earth" (Joshua 7:8–9).

The Lord explained that disobedience cost the defeat at Ai.
The culprit was a soldier named Achan who plundered silver, gold,
and a beautiful robe and hid them under his tent. Once Achan was
dealt with, God told Joshua to attack again. This time Ai fell.

Achan sinned against the Lord. He also caused the death of
thirty-six soldiers in the first attack and the only defeat that Israel
suffered while under Joshua's leadership. A disaster of one form or
another befalls a person who convinces himself or herself that sin
can be hidden and rendered harmless.

*Father, Your Word reminds us that godliness with contentment is
great gain. When we get greedy for things that are not Your will
for us to have, we bring trouble on ourselves. So help us, Lord,
to be content with the good things You have already provided for us.*

Joshua Prays for a Longer Day

Then spake Joshua to the LORD in the day when the LORD
delivered up the Amorites before the children of Israel,
and he said in the sight of Israel, Sun, stand thou still
upon Gibeon; and thou, Moon, in the valley of Ajalon.
JOSHUA 10:12

Town leaders of Gibeon knew the Lord had instructed Joshua to drive everyone from Canaan. They dressed in well-worn clothes and pretended to be travelers from a far country. They asked Joshua to be their ally. Without consulting the Lord, he agreed to a treaty.

Kings of five other cities learned of the alliance and pooled their armies to attack the Gibeonites, who sent word to Joshua, "Come quickly and save us." Joshua agreed to do so, because to dishonor his word would dishonor God as well.

Joshua made an all-night march from his camp at Gilgal. At the appearance of his forces, the five kings and their armies tried to flee. As the battle wore on, Joshua did not want the opposing fighters to slip away in the night. Joshua prayed to the Lord, "Sun, stand thou still upon Gibeon" (Joshua 10:12). And it did. The long day ensured Joshua's victory.

Near the end of his life, Joshua instructed the Israelites to honor God. His rush to form an alliance with Gibeon had embarrassed him. Events in his life showed that fidelity to the Lord is permanent, while worldly alliances are temporary.

How powerful and gracious You are, almighty God!
When our foes surround us, You are our strong
defender. We trust in You.

Deborah Praises God

Hear, O ye kings; give ear, O ye princes; I, even I, will sing unto the Lord; I will sing praise to the Lord God of Israel.
JUDGES 5:3

❧ ─────────────────── ❧

The story of Deborah, the only female judge of Israel, is detailed in Judges 4, and her song of victory praising God is in chapter 5. Together the two chapters paint a dramatic picture of how the ragtag band of Israelites with crude weapons defeated a vastly superior army with nine hundred iron chariots.

Iron chariots were new and fearsome war machines, able to strike as much terror into foot soldiers as modern-day tanks did when they first rumbled across the battlefield. A clue to how God intervened is revealed in Deborah's song: "The clouds also dropped water. . .the highways were unoccupied" (Judges 5:4, 6). The mighty iron chariots of the enemy sank into a quagmire of mud and were rendered useless. The enemy fled the battlefield.

The battle itself occurred because the Israelites forgot all that God had done for them. They became weak and easy prey for Canaanite raiders. When the people asked Deborah for relief, she called her general to lead warriors against the Canaanites. Barak, Deborah's general, refused to act unless she accompanied him, which she did—a brave woman who trusted God.

Thank You, Father, for using people of both genders to do Your work. In Your sight there is neither Jew nor Gentile, slave nor free, male nor female, for we are all one in Christ. Give us all courage to respond to Your calling as Deborah did.

Gideon Prays for His Weak Clan

And Gideon said unto him, Oh my Lord, if the Lord be with us,
why then is all this befallen us? and where be all his miracles which
our fathers told us of, saying, Did not the Lord bring us
up from Egypt? but now the Lord hath forsaken us,
and delivered us into the hands of the Midianites.
Judges 6:13

The Israelites served God throughout the lifetime of Deborah, but then they fell back to the pattern that brought disaster. They would worship false gods and be invaded. In the time of Gideon, the Midianites overran their farms, stole their grain and cattle, and left them with nothing to eat. As described in Judges 6, in desperation, the Israelites cried out to the Lord for help.

An angel appeared to Gideon as he threshed grain inside a winepress to keep his meager harvest hidden from the Midianites. Gideon questioned the angel: "If the Lord be with us, why then is all this befallen us?" (Judges 6:13). Gideon did not expect the reply he received: "Go in this thy might, and thou shalt save Israel from the hand of the Midianites: have not I sent thee?" (verse 14).

"Wherewith shall I save Israel? behold, my family is poor in Manasseh, and I am the least in my father's house" (verse 15). Before the physical challenge with the Midianites, Gideon had to understand the strength for victory was in God's power, not in his skill as a military leader. Gideon accepted the Lord's decision to reduce the size of his army from thirty-two thousand men to only three hundred fighters.

As Gideon's account illustrates, spiritual guidance helps us prepare for victory over physical challenges.

Dear Father, Your Word teaches us that physical training is of some
value, but godliness holds promise for both this life and the life
to come. May we therefore, grow strong in Your Word so that
we will be prepared to fight the battles You call us to face.

Gideon Asks for a Sign

*If now I have found grace in thy sight,
then shew me a sign that thou talkest with me.*
JUDGES 6:17

The angel of the Lord came to Gideon and announced that he was a mighty warrior who would defeat Israel's enemies. Gideon wanted reassurance that the angel spoke for God. Gideon made an offering of meat and unleavened bread. As soon as the angel's staff touched the offering, fire consumed it (see Judges 6).

The Lord now commanded Gideon to tear down his father's altar to the false god Baal and cut down the Asherah pole. Although his father had built the altar, he now came to his son's side against the villagers who threatened to kill Gideon.

As this crisis ended, a much larger one loomed. Israel's enemies once again invaded the country. Gideon called for fighting men from his tribe (Manasseh) and three others. As they assembled, Gideon once again needed reassurance. He asked for a sign, first that fleece would collect dew overnight while the threshing floor remained dry, and the next night the reverse. God answered his request and reassured him.

Gideon's many doubts did not keep him from obeying God. For each of us today, doubt and fear can bring on a troubled mind, but an active faith does what God directs despite our misgivings.

*Father, Your promise is that if we lack wisdom, we should come
to You who gives generously to all without finding fault,
and You will give us wisdom. Thank You, Lord, that
You haven't left us to make decisions on our own.*

Jephthah's Impulsive Prayer for Victory

*Jephthah vowed a vow unto the LORD, and said, If thou shalt
without fail deliver the children of Ammon into mine hands,
then it shall be, that whatsoever cometh forth of the doors
of my house to meet me, when I return in peace from the
children of Ammon, shall surely be the LORD's,
and I will offer it up for a burnt offering.*
JUDGES 11:30–31

Jephthah was troubled from his youth. His mother was a harlot,
and his half brothers—born to his father's wife—drove him away
to make sure he didn't receive any inheritance. After suffering their
rejection, Jephthah joined a gang of worthless thugs.

When war broke out, the men from his country realized
Jephthah could be a valuable asset. They said, "Be our commander.
After we win the war, you can lead us."

Jephthah didn't depend on his own ability or the strength of
Israel's army to fight the battle. He trusted the Lord but made an
impulsive promise to God: "If thou shalt without fail deliver the
children of Ammon into mine hands. . .whatsoever cometh forth
of the doors of my house to meet me, when I return in peace from
the children of Ammon, shall surely be the LORD's, and I will offer
it up for a burnt offering" (Judges 11:30–31).

Imagine Jephthah's horror when his daughter rushed out of
the house to greet him. He was heartbroken over his rash vow, but
he told her about it and said he couldn't go back on his word.

*Thank You, Jesus, for giving Your life to be our ultimate
sacrifice. You eternally eliminated the need for burnt offerings.
Now we offer ourselves as living sacrifices to glorify You.*

Manoah Prays for Instructions

Then Manoah intreated the LORD, and said, O my LORD,
let the man of God which thou didst send come again unto us,
and teach us what we shall do unto the child that shall be born.
JUDGES 13:8

Manoah's wife had been unable to bear children—something that made women of the Bible feel worthless. But God liked to surprise senior citizens with unexpected babies. A man of God came to her, saying, "Behold, thou shalt conceive, and bear a son" (Judges 13:7). He told her not to drink wine or eat anything unclean while she was pregnant and said the child would be dedicated to the Lord his entire life. She believed what he said but didn't realize she was hearing from an angel.

When she told her husband about the experience, he never doubted her but wanted to know how to raise this miraculous child. Judges 13:8 says, "Then Manoah intreated the LORD, and said. . .let the man of God which thou didst send come again unto us, and teach us what we shall do unto the child that shall be born." The angel returned and spoke to Manoah but didn't give specific details about how to care for the child.

Now we know their baby was Samson, the man noted for his tremendous strength. He would become a leader in Israel, delivering them from the Philistines. Even though Samson made some poor choices, God ultimately used him for the good of His people.

Lord, we pray for Your wisdom and instructions,
no matter what You ask us to do. We choose to trust
You even when we don't understand.

Samson Prays for Water

*Thou hast given this great deliverance into the hand
of thy servant: and now shall I die for thirst?*
JUDGES 15:18

God gave Samson amazing strength to overpower the Philistines, who were forever at war against Israel. In one clash, Samson killed a thousand enemies, using only a donkey's jawbone as his weapon. Judges 15:18 tells us what happened after that battle: "He was sore athirst, and called on the LORD, and said, Thou hast given this great deliverance into the hand of thy servant: and now shall I die for thirst, and fall into the hand of the uncircumcised?"

God heard and answered Samson's plea for water: "God clave an hollow place. . .and there came water thereout; and when he had drunk, his spirit came again, and he revived" (Judges 15:19).

Samson's parents probably told him about his miraculous birth and what the angel said concerning his life. He became one of the judges who led the Israelites before they had a king. God took care of Samson, even splitting a rock to provide refreshing water when he was parched. Throughout Samson's life, God continued to work through him to accomplish the things he was created for.

*Heavenly Father, thank You for watching over us all the time.
We ask You to keep us pure so we are able to refresh those
around us with living water that comes from You.*

Samson's Final Request

And Samson called unto the LORD, and said, O Lord God,
remember me, I pray thee, and strengthen me, I pray thee,
only this once, O God, that I may be at once avenged
of the Philistines for my two eyes.
JUDGES 16:28

Samson's parents did all they could to raise their special child to serve God, but Samson made some foolish choices. He was tantalized by Delilah, and his relationship with her became more important than pleasing the Lord. The Philistines used her to destroy him. Delilah pressured him until he told the secret of his remarkable strength, and God allowed him to be captured. The Philistines bound him in chains, gouged out his eyes, and put him in prison.

Later the Philistines held a huge festival in the temple of their god, Dagon. During the celebration, they brought Samson to perform and entertain them.

Then Samson prayed to the Lord, "Lord God, remember me, I pray thee, and strengthen me, I pray thee, only this once, O God, that I may be at once avenged of the Philistines for my two eyes" (Judges 16:28).

Even though Samson wasted his blessings, God answered his final prayer. Samson put his hands on the pillars that supported the temple and pushed. The entire building crashed down, killing everyone. More Philistines died from Samson's last act than he killed in his lifetime.

Dear Lord, we want to spend our lives in obedience,
serving You. But thank You that even though we
make mistakes, You never fail us.

Israelites Pray for Guidance

*And the children of Israel arose, and went up to the house of God,
and asked counsel of God, and said, Which of us shall go up
first to the battle against the children of Benjamin?*
JUDGES 20:18

Several times in the book of Judges we're told, "There was no king in Israel, and everyone did what was right in his own eyes." Sin was rampant.

One night a Levite stopped in a town that belonged to people from the tribe of Benjamin. While the Levite was there, perverted men surrounded the house and almost broke down the door, trying to get to him. We can't comprehend his thinking, but he forced his concubine to go out to them. They abused her all night, and in the morning he found her body at the door of the house.

The Levite sent a gruesome message throughout Israel, seeking revenge against the tribe of Benjamin. At first the plan was just to deal with those who murdered his concubine, but the men from Benjamin wouldn't cooperate. Then the rest of the Israelis joined forces and formed an army of four hundred thousand prepared for battle.

When they met together, they went to the house of God and prayed, "Which of us shall go up first to the battle against the children of Benjamin? And the LORD said, Judah shall go up first" (Judges 20:18). The Israelites looked to God for guidance, and He was gracious to them.

*May we always seek You first, Lord,
and listen to Your words to show us the way.*

Israelites Ask If They Should Fight Their Brothers

And the children of Israel went up and wept before the Lord until even, and asked counsel of the Lord, saying, Shall I go up again to battle against the children of Benjamin my brother?
JUDGES 20:23

Because some men of Benjamin murdered a Levite's concubine, Israel's army demanded justice. The Israelites banded together and battled the evil men. But in the first two days, forty thousand Israelites were killed. They outnumbered their enemy and were fighting for what they believed was right, but the outcome looked grim. Each day they asked God if they should continue.

After the second day of brutal combat, with a tenth of their men dead, they wept before the Lord. "Shall I yet again go out to battle against the children of Benjamin my brother, or shall I cease?" (Judges 20:28). It is easy to understand their discouragement; they questioned the wisdom of fighting these men they considered brothers.

But God answered, "Go up; for to morrow I will deliver them into thine hand" (verse 28). It had to take some major courage to fight the third day, after the slaughter they suffered before. But their prayer was heartfelt, not just a ritual. They asked God because they knew they could do nothing less than obey His directions. They wanted to honor their brothers but seemed to understand that God might be using them to clean sin from the land.

Dear Lord, give us hearts to love and honor others,
but more than that, to do whatever You direct us to do,
even if it goes against what feels right to us.

Israelites Ask about One Missing Tribe

O LORD God of Israel, why is this come to pass in Israel,
that there should be to day one tribe lacking in Israel?
JUDGES 21:3

Israel knew God had to eliminate sin or it would ultimately destroy the entire nation. But instead of feeling euphoric as winners, after the battles against the Benjamites ended, the Israelites grieved for their brothers—the tribe would surely disappear.

Israel's prayer is recorded in Judges 21:3: "Why is this come to pass in Israel, that there should be to day one tribe lacking in Israel?" The next morning they built an altar and sacrificed peace offerings.

Six hundred Benjamites survived and hid in the wilderness, but the men of Israel had sworn not to allow their daughters to marry into that tribe. Without marriage, Benjamin's family would cease to exist. Through some questionable tactics, wives were found for them so the tribe could continue.

If there were no evil, God would never have to resort to radical means to purify His people. But before we question His drastic scheme, consider Jesus. The most extreme method of cleansing sin took Jesus to the cross. For us.

Thank You, Lord, for Your matchless tactic to eliminate sin
that would destroy our lives. May Your salvation
spread to the ends of the earth.

Hannah Prays for a Son

O Lord of hosts, if thou wilt indeed look on the affliction of thine handmaid, and remember me, and not forget thine handmaid, but wilt give unto thine handmaid a man child, then I will give him unto the Lord all the days of his life.
1 SAMUEL 1:11

Hannah felt like a failure. Her husband, Elkanah, cherished and honored her, but she didn't have any children, and in those days, people thought women without children were cursed. Even though Elkanah treated her special, Hannah desperately longed for a son.

Each year, the couple traveled to Shiloh, where they prayed and worshipped the Lord. And Hannah made a vow, saying, "O LORD of hosts, if thou wilt indeed look on the affliction of thine handmaid, and. . .wilt give unto thine handmaid a man child, then I will give him unto the LORD all the days of his life" (1 Samuel 1:11).

She was so distressed, Eli the priest thought she was drunk. When she explained her plight, he said, "Go in peace: and the God of Israel grant thee thy petition that thou hast asked of him" (verse 17).

Could she believe Eli? Did he know what he was talking about? His words must have ignited a glimmer of hope in her heart. We are not sure how old Hannah was, but she had begged for a child for years and had reached a point of despair. After her earnest prayer, it isn't surprising to read that "when the time was come" Hannah gave birth to Samuel (verse 20).

You are magnificent, Lord God. Help us resist thinking that You aren't able to grant our deepest desires. When we love You, our desires will line up perfectly with Your desires for us.

Hannah Rejoices in God

*And Hannah prayed, and said, My heart rejoiceth in the LORD,
mine horn is exalted in the LORD: my mouth is enlarged over
mine enemies; because I rejoice in thy salvation.*
1 SAMUEL 2:1

Hannah's promise, that she would give her son to the Lord may
have seemed impulsive, but she was sincere. When Samuel was
born, Hannah could have rationalized that it didn't really mean
he couldn't remain under her care. Just knowing in her heart that
Samuel belonged to God was surely enough. She was thrilled
with this miraculous child and tenderly cared for him until he was
weaned, probably two or three years.

Then she followed through with her commitment. She took
him to the temple after he was weaned and placed him in Eli's care.
How heart-wrenching it must have been to give her treasure to the
Lord. And it wasn't temporary. She said, "I will give him unto the
LORD all the days of his life" (1 Samuel 1:11).

In spite of her pain, she rejoiced in the blessing. First Samuel
2:1 says, "My heart rejoiceth in the LORD."

Because Hannah relinquished her maternal control over
Samuel, God was able to mold him into the man he was designed
to be. He became the prophet who led Israel throughout his adult
life.

*Thank You, Lord, that we each are designed for the specific
work we are to accomplish. When we fulfill Your plans for us,
we rejoice and our hearts are filled with praise.*

The Blessing of Eli

*And Eli blessed Elkanah and his wife, and said, The Lord give
thee seed of this woman for the loan which is lent to the
Lord. And they went unto their own home.*
1 Samuel 2:20

Hannah's faith is amazing. Her prayer for a son was finally answered—after years of waiting—yet she willingly parted with her precious child. What faith it took!

After giving Samuel to Eli at the temple, she only saw him when she and Elkanah went to Shiloh for an annual sacrifice. Every year she made a little robe for Samuel. Surely those garments were sprinkled with tears as she stitched, making each one a larger size. Her toddler grew into an active little boy, then a teenager, and finally a full-grown man. Hannah must have cherished those moments when they could visit. Eli saw her love for Samuel.

Before they returned home, Eli would bless Elkanah and his wife and ask the Lord to bless them with other children to replace the one they gave to the Lord.

Hannah believed that God rewards those who sincerely seek Him. He blessed her faith by giving her three more sons and two daughters. No one could actually take Samuel's place in Hannah's heart, but these children surely enriched her life. They gave her a daily outlet for motherly love.

*When we willingly give our treasures to You, Lord, You bless us in
return with more than we can imagine. Thank You!*

God Called Samuel

Speak; for thy servant heareth.
1 SAMUEL 3:10

Has the Lord spoken to you? When Samuel was a boy, it was rare for anyone to hear from God. First Samuel 3:1 says, "The word of the LORD was precious in those days; there was no open vision."

One evening Samuel heard a voice call his name. He thought it was Eli, so Samuel ran to see what he needed. Eli told him he hadn't called. This happened three times, and finally Eli realized it was the Lord calling Samuel. We are not sure how old Samuel was at the time, but even though he was young and inexperienced, he was learning to know the Lord's voice.

Samuel went back to his bed. Then, in 1 Samuel 3:10 we are told, "The LORD came, and stood, and called as at other times, Samuel, Samuel. Then Samuel answered, Speak; for thy servant heareth."

As Samuel grew, he learned to recognize God's voice, like sheep that can distinguish their shepherd's speech and intonations. The Lord was with him "and did let none of his words fall to the ground" (verse 19). As God revealed Himself to Samuel, the people realized he was a prophet; they could depend on him to speak what the Lord told him.

May we all become familiar with Your voice, Lord, so we know when You speak to us. Teach us to say what You tell us to say and to keep quiet when we should.

Saul's Rash Oath

Therefore Saul said unto the LORD God of Israel,
Give a perfect lot.
1 SAMUEL 14:41

Israel's army was at a severe disadvantage, with very limited weapons in a fight against the Philistines. But when Jonathan, Saul's son, attacked the enemy, the battle turned.

King Saul had ordered the men not to eat anything all day, with a penalty of death for disobedience. Jonathan didn't know about his father's edict, and when he saw a honeycomb in the woods, he ate a little honey.

That evening Saul asked God, "Shall I go down after the Philistines? Will You deliver them into my hand?" (1 Samuel 14:37, author's paraphrase). But God was silent. Somehow, because of that, Saul knew there was sin in his camp. He called the people together to cast lots and figure out who sinned.

Saul and Jonathan were on one side and the rest of the men on the other. "Therefore Saul said unto the LORD God of Israel, Give a perfect lot. And Saul and Jonathan were taken: but the people escaped" (verse 41).

When Saul asked Jonathan what he had done, Jonathan said, "I did but taste a little honey with the end of the rod that was in mine hand, and, lo, I must die" (verse 43). The rest of the army went against their king's impulsive oath in order to rescue Jonathan—they knew his brave fighting had saved them.

Thank You, Lord, for protecting us when we wear
Your armor of truth and righteousness.

David Asks God for Information

Then said David, O LORD God of Israel. . . . Will the men of Keilah deliver me up into his hand? will Saul come down, as thy servant hath heard?
1 SAMUEL 23:10–11

Saul wanted David dead. It didn't matter that David had always been faithful to him. David's trust in God gave him courage to fight his enemies, and he easily could have killed Saul several times. But he refused to fight against God's anointed, even though Saul was determined to destroy him.

Once when he was hiding, David said, "O LORD God of Israel, thy servant hath certainly heard that Saul seeketh to come to Keilah, to destroy the city for my sake. Will the men of Keilah deliver me up into his hand? will Saul come down, as thy servant hath heard? O LORD God of Israel, I beseech thee, tell thy servant. And the LORD said, He will come down. Then said David, Will the men of Keilah deliver me and my men into the hand of Saul? And the LORD said, They will deliver thee up" (1 Samuel 23:10–12).

For some reason, David didn't ask God to intervene, he just wanted information. So he and his men left and kept moving from place to place. When Saul found out David wasn't there any longer, he saw no need to go, either.

In this case, David's protection was the knowledge he received from the Lord. Because he knew Saul's plan, he was able to escape.

Thank You, Lord, for showing us through this example that sometimes all we need to be safe is to ask for wisdom and then trust You.

David Asks about Defeat of the Amalekites

And David enquired at the LORD, saying,
Shall I pursue after this troop? shall I overtake them?
1 SAMUEL 30:8

While David and his men fought elsewhere, the Amalekites raided Ziklag, where David lived. The enemy captured everyone—all the women and children, plus their herds and flocks. They plundered and burned and left nothing but desolation.

When David's men returned, they wept till they were exhausted, and in their grief they threatened to stone their leader. David's wives and children were among those who were captured, but the men must have blamed him that they weren't home to protect their families. He was in a tight spot, so he strengthened himself in the Lord.

"David enquired at the LORD, saying, Shall I pursue after this troop? Shall I overtake them? And he answered him, Pursue: for thou shalt surely overtake them, and without fail recover all" (1 Samuel 30:8).

When David and his men found the Amalekites, they were drinking and celebrating their conquests, until Israel's army burst in and surprised them. The armies fought all night, and the next day David's troops won the battle. They recovered what had been taken—their wives and children and everything else the Amalekites seized.

Lord, we ask You to show us Your great and marvelous power.
We don't realize what You can accomplish until we are desperate
and have nowhere else to turn. Then we understand
that all our victories come from You.

David Expresses His Grief
for Jonathan and Saul

The beauty of Israel is slain upon thy high places:
how are the mighty fallen!
2 SAMUEL 1:19

Jonathan and David's relationship was deeper than most brothers; their souls were knit together. That is amazing, considering that Saul, Jonathan's father, resented everything David did and desperately tried to destroy him.

At one point, Jonathan presented David with his royal robe, armor, and weapons. In other words, Jonathan stripped himself of his position—next in line for the throne. There was apparently no competitive attitude between them. When David received word that Saul and Jonathan were killed in battle, his grief was intense for both men.

Besides keeping him safe from Saul's attacks, God gave David grace to forgive Saul, so David's conscience was clear at this time of mourning.

David composed a lengthy song of lament and taught it to his followers. Part of it says, "Saul and Jonathan were lovely and pleasant in their lives, and in their death they were not divided: they were swifter than eagles, they were stronger than lions" (2 Samuel 1:23). The song reflects David's strength and unfailing friendship. No wonder he was called a man after God's own heart.

Lord, give us tender hearts that have no room for resentment
and bitterness. Make us quick to forgive, always looking
for the best in those around us.

David's Requests That His House Endure

*Therefore now let it please thee to bless the house of thy servant,
that it may continue for ever before thee.*
2 SAMUEL 7:29

King David was a mighty warrior. He proved himself in battle over and over. Yet the Bible says he questioned the Lord. "Who am I, O Lord GOD? and what is my house, that thou hast brought me hitherto?" (2 Samuel 7:18).

David knew he was totally dependent on the Lord and that God determined his future. David made some huge mistakes, but God saw his heart and knew he yearned to glorify the Lord.

David prayed, "Therefore now let it please thee to bless the house of thy servant, that it may continue for ever before thee: for thou, O Lord GOD, hast spoken it: and with thy blessing let the house of thy servant be blessed for ever" (verse 29).

We don't know if David realized the Messiah would come through his descendants. Looking at his words from this side of Christ's appearance, we know his prayer was answered in Jesus. "He shall be great, and shall be called the Son of the Highest: and the Lord God shall give unto him the throne of his father David" (Luke 1:32). Through Jesus, David's kingdom continues forever.

*Thank You, Father, for seeing more in us than we see—
You see eternity. Let us magnify Your name forever!*

David's Song of Praise

*The God of my rock; in him will I trust: he is my shield,
and the horn of my salvation, my high tower, and my refuge,
my saviour; thou savest me from violence.*
2 SAMUEL 22:3

Whether David was desperately fleeing from Saul or trying to escape when enemy nations were after him, he always glorified God for saving him. David was a mighty warrior, but he understood that without the Lord on his side, he would have been defeated.

We can hear David's voice in many of the psalms. His prayers for guidance, for relief, and for safety echo in our hearts when we face trials. David encountered persecution and rebellion, even from people he trusted. He cried for help, but he never lost confidence in the Lord who could rescue him. He repented whenever he sinned, and depended on God to forgive even his worst wickedness. His praise soared as he remembered times when God delivered him from certain defeat.

In 2 Samuel 22:6–7 David called out, "The sorrows of hell compassed me about; the snares of death prevented me; in my distress I called upon the LORD, and cried to my God: and he did hear my voice out of his temple, and my cry did enter into his ears." And God responded to David's cry.

*Lord, help us grow and learn by joining David's praise
and prayers as we soak up the power of his psalms.*

David Praises God's Justice

For thou art my lamp, O LORD:
and the LORD will lighten my darkness.
2 SAMUEL 22:29

God's justice system is almost beyond our comprehension. Sometimes we don't even like the way He treats people with amazing mercy. We tend to think justice means we should deal with the bad guys the same way they dish out abuse to others. A murderer, thief, or any other brutal person doesn't deserve mercy. Most of the people in David's day thought that way. It was the standard under the old covenant, before Jesus ushered in a new way of thinking.

As a king, David sometimes dealt out quick, no-nonsense judgments against the malicious and underhanded. Other times he showed more mercy than anyone expected. Surrounding nations learned to fear and respect him and his leadership methods.

After God delivered him from his enemies, David composed a beautiful song of praise. One verse from it says: "With the merciful thou wilt shew thyself merciful, and with the upright man thou wilt shew thyself upright" (2 Samuel 22:26).

David was truly an amazing leader. When his army was at war, he was in the midst of the battle. He set an example for his people. And even when he sinned, he had a heart for God's ways.

Lord God, we rejoice because of Your mercy and Your promise
to forget our sins. Help us be merciful and upright
so that our attitudes glorify You.

David Praises God for Victory

For thou hast girded me with strength to battle:
them that rose up against me hast thou subdued under me.
2 SAMUEL 22:40

David knew God delivered him and made him successful. Part of his victory song says, "The LORD liveth; and blessed be my rock; and exalted be the God of the rock of my salvation. It is God that avengeth me, and that bringeth down the people under me" (2 Samuel 22:47–48).

David battled against people, but he realized his fight was not only with men. The real enemy was the evil one who wants to destroy God's kingdom. The nations that served other gods raged against the Israelites because of their belief in the one true God. The devil was at work in those foreign nations, so there was much more at stake than merely seeing who had the strongest army.

Satan is still our worst enemy.

The closing verse of David's victory song is this: "He is the tower of salvation for his king: and sheweth mercy to his anointed, unto David, and to his seed for evermore" (verse 51). That gives us so much to consider. Jesus Christ is David's descendant who was to come. He lives forever and will return.

Heavenly Father, we too ask You to make us victorious against
the enemy who wants to destroy Your children. Help us realize
how vital it is never to compromise with the real adversary.

David Asks God to Remove His Guilt

And David said unto the LORD, I have sinned greatly in that I have done: and now, I beseech thee, O LORD, take away the iniquity of thy servant; for I have done very foolishly.
2 SAMUEL 24:10

For some reason, David was determined to conduct a census, even though his advisers discouraged the plan. He wanted to count the fighting men to learn the strength of his army. That surprises us because of the many times David praised God for defeating enemy nations. The census violated Israel's relationship with Yahweh, their true strength.

They counted over a million "valiant men that drew the sword" (see 2 Samuel 24:9). Apparently he regretted it almost immediately. Second Samuel 24:10 says, "David's heart smote him after that he had numbered the people," and then he promptly begged God to remove his guilt.

David's heart broke. He instantly repented, but sometimes we must suffer consequences for our actions. The Lord offered him three options, and David chose to "let us fall now into the hand of the LORD" (verse 14). As a result, Israel experienced a terribly destructive three-day plague.

Dear Lord, when we sin, we want to be as eager to ask for Your forgiveness as David. Let our hearts beat as one with Yours.

David Pleads for His People

Lo, I have sinned, and I have done wickedly: but these sheep,
what have they done? let thine hand, I pray thee,
be against me, and against my father's house.
2 SAMUEL 24:17

The plague that struck Israel as a result of David's sin killed seventy thousand people, from Dan to Beersheba. David was horrified. Imagine how devastating it must have been, knowing he was to blame for such a terrible calamity.

Apparently David witnessed an angel who was about to destroy Jerusalem. Second Samuel 24:17 says, "David spake unto the LORD when he saw the angel that smote the people." Then David asked God to cause all of the consequences to fall on him and his family, and he prayed for protection of the innocent people. So God restrained the angel.

A prophet named Gad instructed David to build an altar at the site where the angel appeared, and David didn't hesitate. He did as he was told. The owner of a threshing floor where the altar was to be erected offered to give it to David, along with animals for a sacrifice, but David refused the gift. He bought the property and the sacrifice, saying, "Nay; but I will surely buy it of thee at a price: neither will I offer burnt offerings unto the LORD my God of that which doth cost me nothing" (verse 24). Verse 25 tells us David offered sacrifices and the Lord listened to his prayers. The plague was withdrawn from the land.

Thank You, Lord, for always being ready to respond
to a repentant sinner's earnest prayer.

Solomon Prays for Discernment

*And now, O LORD my God, thou hast made thy servant king
instead of David my father: and I am but a little child:
I know not how to go out or come in.*
1 KINGS 3:7

Solomon is noted for his wisdom, but when he became king he felt completely unprepared. Although his father, David, had groomed him to rule Israel, Solomon was inexperienced in the politics and intricacies involved.

He faced a major challenge even before he was crowned. His half brother Adonijah gathered a following and claimed to be king, against their father's wishes. King David was old, but when Bathsheba, Solomon's mother, and Nathan, a prophet, told David what was happening, David exerted his royal authority. With great pageantry, he presented Solomon to the people as their new king.

Solomon knew he would only be a good ruler if he depended on God's supernatural intervention. He prayed, "Give therefore thy servant an understanding heart to judge thy people, that I may discern between good and bad: for who is able to judge this thy so great a people?" (1 Kings 3:9).

Because he didn't ask for selfish things—riches, long life, or destruction of his enemies—God was pleased, and granted Solomon more wisdom than anyone before or after him. God also gave him tremendous wealth, but He expected Solomon to stay true to Him as David had.

*You are marvelous, Lord God! You give us more than we can
imagine, and all You want from us is our love.*

Solomon Praises the Lord
for Keeping His Promise

Blessed be the LORD God of Israel, which spake with his mouth
unto David my father, and hath with his hand fulfilled it.
1 KINGS 8:15

One of the main things on Solomon's to-do list after he became king was to build a temple in Jerusalem. That had been in David's heart, but God told him Solomon would fulfill the dream. Solomon finished what his father started, accumulating everything he needed for this huge project. He hired the best artists and craftsmen to cut stones, create the furnishings, weave fine cloth, and blend fragrant incense.

When the work was completed, priests brought the ark of the covenant into the Holy of Holies, in the heart of the temple. And the glory of the Lord filled the place! God's presence was so tangible, the priests could no longer minister. They knew He was right there in their midst.

Solomon was moved to exalt the Lord because He kept His commitment. Solomon said, "The LORD hath performed his word that he spake, and I am risen up in the room of David my father, and sit on the throne of Israel, as the LORD promised, and have built an house for the name of the LORD God of Israel" (1 Kings 8:20).

Holy God, we are living temples and long to be full of Your
presence, just as Solomon's temple was filled with Your glory.

Solomon Dedicates the Temple

*Will God indeed dwell on the earth? behold, the heaven
and heaven of heavens cannot contain thee; how much less
this house that I have builded?*
1 KINGS 8:27

Solomon's wisdom and immense wealth were known worldwide.
People came from far countries to be his guests and give him gifts,
to see his treasures and learn from him.

He directed the building of an exquisite temple. It sparkled
with gold, overlaid on the finest cedar. Artisans created solid gold
candleholders and cherubim. Expensive fabric was woven for the
veil that separated the Holy of Holies. Every detail was prepared to
exact specifications, and the building was completed.

At the temple dedication, Solomon must have been struck by
the enormity of the occasion and his own humanity. He erected a
house for God, yet he realized even the heavens can't contain His
splendor. He prayed to God in 1 Kings 8:29 "that thine eyes may
be open toward this house night and day, even toward the place of
which thou hast said, My name shall be there: that thou mayest
hearken unto the prayer which thy servant shall make toward this
place."

Solomon may have been so busy with preparations for the
temple that he lost track of what it actually signified. It was located
in Israel, where Solomon was king, but it didn't belong to him. It
was totally for God's name.

*Father God, You are too magnificent to be kept in temples
or cathedrals. Help us continually be aware of Your
limitless presence, power, and love.*

Solomon's Plea for Israel

Then hear thou in heaven their prayer and their supplication,
and maintain their cause. If they sin against thee, (for there is
no man that sinneth not,) and thou be angry with them,
and deliver them to the enemy, so that they carry them
away captives unto the land of the enemy, far or near.
1 KINGS 8:45–46

Solomon knew he would make mistakes, and he had no unrealistic expectations about the rest of Israel. The entire population would need God's forgiveness, over and over. Most people won't rule a nation, like Solomon, but whether we are leaders or servants, we all sin. We are hopelessly lost without God's merciful forgiveness.

Solomon's prayers at the dedication ceremony covered any number of specific situations. He knew sin could cause defeats in battle, sickness, famine, and other catastrophes. And he believed in God's loving-kindness to respond with healing when people repented.

Solomon prayed, "What prayer and supplication soever be made by any man, or by all thy people Israel, which shall know every man the plague of his own heart, and spread forth his hands toward this house: then hear thou in heaven thy dwelling place, and forgive, and do, and give to every man according to his ways, whose heart thou knowest; (for thou, even thou only, knowest the hearts of all the children of men;) that they may fear thee all the days that they live in the land which thou gavest unto our fathers" (1 Kings 8:38–40).

Like Solomon, we come to You humbly, Lord, and ask You to forgive
our sin. You are our hope, our healing, and our salvation.

Solomon Prays for Foreigners

Hear thou in heaven thy dwelling place,
and do according to all that the stranger calleth to thee for.
1 KINGS 8:43

Many people from other nations visited Israel, and at the temple dedication Solomon prayed for them also. "Moreover concerning a stranger, that is not of thy people Israel, but cometh out of a far country for thy name's sake; (for they shall hear of thy great name, and of thy strong hand, and of thy stretched out arm;) when he shall come and pray toward this house; hear thou in heaven thy dwelling place, and do according to all that the stranger calleth to thee for: that all people of the earth may know thy name, to fear thee, as do thy people Israel; and that they may know that this house, which I have builded, is called by thy name" (1 Kings 8:41–43).

Solomon understood that the God of Israel would welcome people from other lands. He was not limited to hearing only the prayers of Hebrews. In that way, all nations would know God's greatness, the same as the people of Israel.

Thank You, Lord, that even though Solomon's temple is no
longer standing in Jerusalem, You are available to all people,
from every place on earth, all the time. You welcome us and
hear our prayers, no matter where we are
or what language we speak.

Solomon's Desire for Israel's Faithfulness

The LORD our God be with us, as he was with our fathers:
let him not leave us, nor forsake us: that he may incline our
hearts unto him, to walk in all his ways, and to keep his
commandments, and his statutes, and his judgments,
which he commanded our fathers.
1 KINGS 8:57–58

Solomon knelt before the altar with his hands lifted up to heaven as he prayed for Israel. Though he was a king, he humbled himself in worship, setting an example for his people and for us.

Then he stood and blessed all those who had gathered together. His faith was grounded and settled, due to the teaching he received from his father. When the temple was dedicated, Solomon's beliefs were strong and he yearned for all Israel to stay true to the God of their fathers.

He asked God to watch over the people. "That all the people of the earth may know that the LORD is God, and that there is none else. Let your heart therefore be perfect with the LORD our God, to walk in his statutes, and to keep his commandments, as at this day" (1 Kings 8:60–61).

We know from the rest of Solomon's story that his own faith faltered. He made poor choices later in life and faced inevitable consequences. People fail, but God never does. Every promise of His comes about.

Heavenly Father, we ask You to keep us in Your tender
care always so that our faith stays strong and
we never slip away from You.

Elijah Prays for a Widow's Son

O LORD my God, I pray thee,
let this child's soul come into him again.
1 KINGS 17:21

Elijah, one of the most famous prophets in Israel's history, lived during the reign of Ahab. This king was vile and provoked God's anger more than all the kings before him. So the Lord instructed Elijah to pronounce a curse on the land. At God's command, there would be no rain.

He told Elijah to hide near a brook where God would care for him. But eventually the brook dried up and God directed him to the home of a poor widow. She was destitute but fixed a meal for Elijah and her son, using the last bit of food in her house. Because of her generosity, she experienced a miracle; her food supply never ran out.

Sometime later her son became sick and died. The woman pleaded with Elijah to help. First Kings 17:20–21 says, "He cried unto the LORD, and said, O LORD my God, hast thou also brought evil upon the widow with whom I sojourn, by slaying her son? And he stretched himself upon the child three times, and cried unto the LORD, and said, O LORD my God, I pray thee, let this child's soul come into him again." Elijah kept praying until God revived the boy. Imagine the joy they felt!

Dear Lord, we want to be generous with everything
You give and trust You to supply all we need.
Help us continually seek more of You.

Elijah Prays for Fire

Elijah the prophet came near, and said, LORD God of Abraham,
Isaac, and of Israel, let it be known this day that thou art God in
Israel, and that I am thy servant, and that I have done all these
things at thy word. Hear me, O LORD, hear me, that this people
may know that thou art the LORD God, and that thou
hast turned their heart back again.
1 KINGS 18:36–37

Elijah was zealous for God and appalled by the Israelites who started worshipping other gods. He gathered the people together at Mount Carmel and accused them of faltering between two beliefs. Then he challenged 450 prophets of Baal to test their god. They were to prepare a bull for sacrifice without lighting a fire. Elijah would do the same. Each side would pray for fire to come from heaven to devour their sacrifice.

The prophets of Baal cried out to their god. They danced and shouted and cut themselves to get Baal's attention. There was no response.

That evening Elijah took twelve stones, representing Israel's tribes. He built an altar with a trench around its base. He laid the sacrifice on it and poured three large pots of water over it. Then he prayed, and fire burst from heaven: "Then the fire of the LORD fell, and consumed the burnt sacrifice, and the wood, and the stones, and the dust, and licked up the water that was in the trench. And when all the people saw it, they fell on their faces: and they said, The LORD, he is the God; the LORD, he is the God" (1 Kings 18:38–39).

Almighty Lord, we offer ourselves, broken and contrite, to You.
Thank You for accepting everyone who sincerely comes to You.

Elijah Prays That He Might Die

O Lord, take away my life;
for I am not better than my fathers.
1 KINGS 19:4

Elijah experienced an awesome miracle when he challenged the prophets of Baal. Immediately after that, he ordered their execution. King Ahab's wife, Jezebel, was furious and planned to kill Elijah. So what did he do? He ran for his life.

First Kings 19:4 tells us, "He himself went a day's journey into the wilderness, and came and sat down under a juniper tree: and he requested for himself that he might die; and said, It is enough; now, O LORD, take away my life; for I am not better than my fathers."

It is amazing that a man of such strong faith could become despondent so quickly. Why didn't he just ask God to eliminate his enemies? It must be a trait of human nature to feel isolated and miserable after a tremendous success.

In the wilderness, an angel brought food and water two different days—another miracle. Afterward Elijah journeyed through the vast Negev desert for forty days. Even today all you see in every direction is sandy soil with a few scraggly bushes scattered here and there. Although he was completely isolated, he remained faithful to God.

Dear Lord, give us courage when we feel tired, weak,
and alone. Remind us that we are righteous because of
Christ Jesus. We yearn to stay faithful to You always.

Elijah Laments His Situation

*And, behold, the word of the LORD came to him, and he said unto him,
What doest thou here, Elijah? And he said, I have been very jealous
for the LORD God of hosts: for the children of Israel have forsaken
thy covenant, thrown down thine altars, and slain thy
prophets with the sword; and I, even I only, am left;
and they seek my life, to take it away.*
1 KINGS 19:9–10

Elijah experienced two great spiritual victories—he defeated the
prophets of Baal and received an answer to his prayer for rain. God
delivered on his promise and honored Elijah's obedience. Instead
of celebration and increased faith, Jezebel's threat to kill him sent
him running for his life.

It is not unusual to become emotionally and physically exhausted
after a spiritual battle. Even after witnessing God's great display of
faithfulness and miraculous power, Elijah let his emotions get the
best of him. When God asked him what he was doing, he responded
that he alone remained true to God, when in fact he was not alone.

Just as he did with Elijah, the enemy of your soul wants to
convince you that you are isolated and alone in hopes of keeping
you from fulfilling your purpose. Run to God and listen for Him to
encourage you to press on.

> *Heavenly Father, thank You for speaking to us as You did
> Elijah and encouraging us to know we are not done yet.
> You will fulfill Your purpose for our lives.*

Elisha Prays, "Let Him See"

*And Elisha prayed, and said, LORD, I pray thee, open his eyes,
that he may see. And the LORD opened the eyes of the young
man; and he saw: and, behold, the mountain was full
of horses and chariots of fire round about Elisha.*
2 KINGS 6:17

Aram and Israel were at war. Elisha repeatedly warned the king of Israel ahead of time of the enemy's plans. The king of Aram flew into a rage when he discovered the prophet knew his plans and shared them with his king. He found out where Elisha was and surrounded his city with chariots and horses.

Elisha's servant got up early the next morning to discover the enemy positioned around his city ready to attack. When Elisha saw his servant's fear, he told him not to be afraid because there were more with them than the number of the army standing ready to do harm. Then Elisha asked God to open his servant's eyes to see what Elisha already knew. God opened the servant's eyes to reveal a mighty heavenly army on Israel's side.

Faith expects God to be at work behind the scenes. When the situation seems impossible, remember that your heavenly Father has more than enough resources to provide for you and protect you.

*Father, forgive us for the times when our faith falls short.
Open our eyes to see Your hand at work in our lives.
Help us trust You to protect and keep us.*

Elisha Prays for the Blinded Army

*And when they came down to him, Elisha prayed unto the LORD,
and said, Smite this people, I pray thee, with blindness.
And he smote them with blindness according to the word of Elisha. . . .
And it came to pass, when they were come into Samaria, that Elisha
said, LORD, open the eyes of these men, that they may see.
And the LORD opened their eyes, and they saw; and,
behold, they were in the midst of Samaria.*

2 KINGS 6:18, 20

Elisha supernaturally knew the Aramean king's battle plans and informed the king of Israel, allowing Israel to stay a step ahead. The king of Aram was furious. He tracked Elisha down and hoped to kill him. Instead, Elisha asked God to blind his army. Once the army was blinded, Elisha told them this was not the city they were looking for and convinced them to follow him to the right place.

He took them into Samaria, Israel's capital city, and then asked God to open their eyes. When their sight returned, they found themselves within the city of their enemy. The king of Israel asked Elisha, "Shall I smite them?" (2 Kings 6:21). Elisha instructed the king to feed them and then let them return to their king. The king of Israel prepared a feast for them, fed them, and then let them go home.

For a season, the people of Aram left Israel alone. God provided supernatural protection in answer to Elisha's prayers again. God's miraculous intervention could not be denied by the enemy or by God's people.

*Lord, thank You for Your protection and provision.
When we find ourselves in trouble, may we look to
You and no one else for the answers we need.*

King Hezekiah's Call for Rescue

*Now therefore, O LORD our God, I beseech thee, save thou us
out of his hand, that all the kingdoms of the earth may
know that thou art the LORD God, even thou only.*

2 KINGS 19:19

Hezekiah, king of Judah, led a nation positioned between two
great world powers—Assyria and Egypt. When Hezekiah received
his crown, Assyria had a stronghold in Judah, giving their king,
Sennacherib, economic and military advantage over his adversaries
because of Judah's position as a major intersection for trade. Unlike
his father, King Ahaz, Hezekiah cultivated his relationship with
God and trusted Him above all else.

Sennacherib sent a message to Hezekiah demanding
surrender, and immediately Hezekiah went to the Lord in prayer.
He sent messengers to ask the prophet Isaiah for advice. With
bold reverence, King Hezekiah acknowledged God's authority and
power and asked God to deliver Judah out of the Assyrian king's
hand so that all the earth would know He is God. Isaiah prophesied
Sennacherib's fall, and that very night the angel of the Lord put
185,000 from the Assyrian army to death and Sennacherib left
Judah alone.

Hezekiah's faith is evidenced by his strong prayer life, desire to
obey God, and willingness to take action.

*God, You are the one and only Deliverer! You have rescued us
from so much. We have faith and confidence that You will
never fail us. When we call on You, You will answer us.
You are always faithful to rescue us.*

Hezekiah's Desire for More Life

I beseech thee, O LORD, remember now how I have walked before thee in truth and with a perfect heart, and have done that which is good in thy sight. And Hezekiah wept sore. And it came to pass, afore Isaiah was gone out into the middle court, that the word of the LORD came to him, saying. . .I have heard thy prayer, I have seen thy tears: behold, I will heal thee. . . . And I will add unto thy days fifteen years.
2 KINGS 20:3–6

Hezekiah was deathly ill. The Bible doesn't say it, but perhaps when Isaiah the prophet showed up, he hoped for good news. Instead, Isaiah's message for him from God was to put his house in order because he was going to die.

When Hezekiah heard the news, he turned his face to the wall and prayed. Maybe Isaiah was still standing there when he rolled toward the wall and prayed to God. Through tears, he reminded God of his faithful obedience. He is recorded as Judah's only king to remain true to God for one hundred years (732–640 BC) in Judah's history.

Before Isaiah left the palace, the Lord spoke another message for Hezekiah. God heard Hezekiah's prayer, provided instruction, and gave him a promise of fifteen more years of life.

Heavenly Father, our times are in Your hands. You know every day of our lives and how they will play out. Give us strength and wisdom to serve You all the days of our lives.

Jabez Invites God to His Center

*And Jabez called on the God of Israel, saying, Oh that thou
wouldest bless me indeed, and enlarge my coast, and that thine
hand might be with me, and that thou wouldest keep me
from evil, that it may not grieve me! And God
granted him that which he requested.*
1 CHRONICLES 4:10

Jabez's story is extremely short—told with only two verses in the
entire Bible but packed with powerful wisdom. First, Jabez was
more honorable than his brothers were. None of his brothers, his
father, nor his mother are mentioned by name in the Bible.

His father didn't even name him, which was the custom of
the day. His mother named him Jabez because his birth caused
her much pain. Imagine that each time someone spoke his name it
reminded them of hurt, sorrow, or pain. Jabez rose above his name
and inquired of the Lord—and his prayer is what he is remembered
for today.

He did not ask God to change his name as He had done for
his forefathers, Abram and Jacob. Instead, Jabez invited God to
become the center of his life—to be with him in all he did. He
asked the Lord to bless him, increase him financially ("enlarge my
coast"), and to keep him from harm. Jabez's story ends abruptly by
simply acknowledging that God granted his request.

*Lord, we invite You to be the center of our lives.
Please be with us in everything we do.*

David Rejoices, Giving Back to God

Wherefore David blessed the LORD before all the congregation: and David said, Blessed be thou, LORD God of Israel our father, for ever and ever. Thine, O LORD is the greatness, and the power, and the glory, and the victory, and the majesty: for all that is in the heaven and in the earth is thine; thine is the kingdom, O LORD, and thou art exalted as head above all.

1 CHRONICLES 29:10–11

King David carried a desire to build a house for God in his heart for years, but it was not God's plan for David to build it. His prayer in 1 Chronicles 29:10–20 records his heartfelt praise for the overwhelming response of gifts for building God a temple. So he prepared everything that would be needed for his son, Solomon, to build it. He thanked God for blessing the people and rejoiced as they gave back to God what was already His. David was pleased to see his people worship God with their money—reminding God and the people that everything they called their own came from God's hand.

David thanked God for the demonstration of unreserved devotion God's chosen people displayed. He prayed for Solomon, the next king who would lead His people, to desire to live his life each day committed first to serving God more than anything else.

Heavenly Father, thank You for the blessings You have poured out in our lives. Everything we have and all that we are, You gave us. We pray that our hearts will be tender and generous toward You as You direct us to give to Your good works.

Asa's Prayer for Victory over the Cushites

And Asa cried unto the Lord his God, and said, Lord,
it is nothing with thee to help, whether with many, or with them
that have no power: help us, O Lord our God; for we rest on thee,
and in thy name we go against this multitude. O Lord,
thou art our God; let no man prevail against thee.
2 Chronicles 14:11

The first ten years of Asa's reign as king of Judah is marked by peace because he chose to follow God's commands. King Asa removed idols of the foreign gods from Judah and commanded his people to pursue the God of Abraham, Isaac, and Israel. He took the opportunity in times of peace to build up Judah's defenses and prepare for the battles before they made themselves known.

When the vast army of the Cushites marched on Judah, King Asa realized they were powerless against them, but instead of giving up, he asked God to do what only He could do—give Judah victory. With the Lord on his side, King Asa sent his men to meet the Cushites, and the Lord struck them down. Judah pursued the Cushites and took spoils of the villages they came across, returning home with sheep, camels, and goats.

Lord, we choose to follow You—to be obedient to Your Word
and Your will. Fill us and our households with peace,
and give us victory in all we do.

Jehoshaphat Calls on God's Power

And said, O LORD God of our fathers, art not thou God in heaven?
and rulest not thou over all the kingdoms of the heathen?
and in thine hand is there not power and might, so that none
is able to withstand thee? Art not thou our God, who didst drive
out the inhabitants of this land before thy people Israel,
and gavest it to the seed of Abraham thy friend for ever?
2 CHRONICLES 20:6–7

Jehoshaphat, king of Judah, learned that a great army was coming to war against him and his people. Instead of looking to man, he went to God for help and declared a fast for Judah. He asked his people to join him as they took time to consider their sin and to ask God for help.

Jehoshaphat had the support of his people as they focused on God. He committed the situation to God. He asked God for favor because they belonged to God—his people were God's chosen people. He reminded himself of God's promises and recognized that victory would not come to him through his own wisdom, knowledge, or strategic battle planning—victory would not be his—except by God's power.

God, help us recognize that we are not in control.
The power to win life's battles comes from Your power.
Give us strength to draw on Your ability instead of our own.

Ezra Gives All Credit to God

*Blessed be the LORD God of our fathers, which hath put such a thing as
this in the king's heart, to beautify the house of the LORD which is in
Jerusalem: and hath extended mercy unto me before the king,
and his counsellors, and before all the king's mighty princes.
And I was strengthened as the hand of the LORD my God
was upon me, and I gathered together out
of Israel chief men to go up with me.*
EZRA 7:27–28

Ezra served in Babylon as a scribe and teacher among the exiles
and diplomat to King Artaxerxes. A desire burned in his heart to
return to his homeland—Jerusalem—and he wanted to take as
many of the Israelites as he could with him. The first group of exiles
had returned to Jerusalem eighty years earlier to rebuild the temple.
He needed the king of Persia's support to do so. A letter from King
Artaxerxes provided safe passage in the case of opposition during
their four-month journey home.

When the king granted Ezra's request and provided the letter
that would carry him and approximately two thousand of God's
people home, he gave all the credit to God. He realized it was not
attained on his own abilities, but that God had actually changed
the king's heart in favor of Ezra's request.

*Lord, thank You for Your favor on our lives. You speak to
the hearts of others on our behalf. We give You
credit for every blessing!*

Ezra's Prayer Moves a Nation

*And after all that is come upon us for our evil deeds, and for our
great trespass, seeing that thou our God hast punished us less than
our iniquities deserve. . .wouldest not thou be angry with us till thou
hadst consumed us, so that there should be no remnant nor escaping?
O LORD God of Israel, thou art righteous: for we remain yet escaped,
as it is this day: behold, we are before thee in our trespasses:
for we cannot stand before thee because of this.*

EZRA 9:13–15

Upon his return to Jerusalem, Ezra found that the people had married pagan women—something God commanded them not to do. God desired for them to remain committed to Him, and intermarriage affected them spiritually because it brought idol worship into their homes.

Ezra stood in the gap for the people. He acknowledged their sins as his own. Although he had not married a pagan, he accepted that he was not without sin. He acknowledged the seriousness of sin and the impact sin has, not only on the one sinning but also on those around him or her. He continued by thanking God for His love and mercy toward His people even though they had done nothing to deserve it.

Ezra's public display of repentance and humility moved people. He modeled a repentant heart, causing the people to declare their unfaithfulness and recommit to their covenant with God.

*Lord, sin is serious and something we do not want to take
lightly. Help us remember that our actions speak louder
than words. Give us the courage to be examples for others.*

Nehemiah Follows God with Patience

Now these are thy servants and thy people, whom thou hast redeemed by thy great power, and by thy strong hand. O LORD, I beseech thee, let now thine ear be attentive to the prayer of thy servant, and to the prayer of thy servants, who desire to fear thy name: and prosper, I pray thee, thy servant this day, and grant him mercy in the sight of this man. For I was the king's cupbearer.
NEHEMIAH 1:10–11

A passion for his homeland rose up from within Nehemiah's heart when he heard about the depleted condition of Jerusalem's wall. A city wall in Nehemiah's day was as critical to life as electricity and running water are today. The strength of a city wall determined the level of security and safety for those who lived there.

Nehemiah went to God in prayer, asked God for direction, and then waited patiently for an opportunity. Although waiting can be hard, Nehemiah's patience paid off. The king noticed Nehemiah's sadness and asked what was wrong. At first, Nehemiah was afraid because it was dangerous to show sorrow in the presence of the king. He pressed through his fear and told the king his sad news. The king responded with compassion upon hearing about the walls of Jerusalem and gave Nehemiah permission to go and rebuild his city's walls.

Thank You, God, for the passion You have placed in our hearts. Help us respond with patience and take action according to Your timetable.

Nehemiah's Prayer to Face the Opposition

*For they all made us afraid, saying, Their hands shall
be weakened from the work, that it be not done.
Now therefore, O God, strengthen my hands.*
NEHEMIAH 6:9

The opposition to rebuilding the wall of Jerusalem was not new.
Once Nehemiah arrived, those opposing the wall restoration
challenged him immediately. Those who opposed the wall builders
were foreigners who settled into the land when the Israelites were
taken into exile and Israelites who returned before Nehemiah
and established lucrative businesses. A new wall not only meant a
revitalized community but also a nation ready to defend itself from
those outside the walls.

In addition to physical attacks to tear down what was built
each day, there were accusations, rumors, and attempts to delay
work with requests for negotiations with other leaders. Letters
from King Artaxerxes gave Nehemiah the power and authority
to rebuild the walls and fortify the city. He refused to give in to
any opposition while encouraging his people to defend and protect
their assigned section of the wall as they worked. He took on his
assignment from God, refused to give in to the naysayers, and
prayed for God's strength to face the opposition. He supernaturally
completed the wall in fifty-two days!

*Heavenly Father, thank You for the assignments You have given us.
Forgive us where we have failed. We ask for Your strength
to face the opposition and supernaturally complete the task.*

Israel's Confessions to the Forgiving God

*But they and our fathers dealt proudly, and hardened their necks,
and hearkened not to thy commandments, and refused to obey,
neither were mindful of thy wonders that thou didst among them;
but hardened their necks, and in their rebellion appointed a
captain to return to their bondage: but thou art a God ready
to pardon, gracious and merciful, slow to anger, and of
great kindness, and forsookest them not.*

NEHEMIAH 9:16–17

This long prayer of confession of the sins of Israel in Nehemiah 9:5–38 served to remind the people of God's great mercy and unfailing love—a love He continued to demonstrate in spite of their continued rebellion and sin against God's commands. The verbal confession of sins spoke of their journey and the great promises God had given them, if only they would honor the covenant He made with them as sons and daughters of Abraham.

A time of reflection to carefully consider past mistakes, personal history, and God's faithfulness gave God's people an understanding of their heritage of faith. Since they didn't have printed Bibles to read on their own, verbal assemblies like this gave them answers to why God allowed them to live as slaves in their own country.

*Lord, we never want to take You for granted. Thank You for
the many blessings You have given us. May our hearts always
be tender toward You to confess our sin and honor You.*

Nehemiah Reestablishes What Is Right

Remember me, O my God, concerning this, and wipe not out my good deeds that I have done for the house of my God, and for the offices thereof. . . . Remember me, O my God, for good.
NEHEMIAH 13:14, 31

Nehemiah spent twelve years in Jerusalem before returning to Babylon. He again asked King Artaxerxes for permission to return to Jerusalem, which the king granted. His heart fell when he heard that Eliashib, the priest in charge of the storerooms of God, had married the daughter of Tobiah, an Ammorite, and given Tobiah his own room in the house of God where grain offerings, incense, temple articles, and tithes once were stored.

Nehemiah found out that the Levites had not been giving tithes and had therefore left the temple to work in the fields. The people were working and trading on the Sabbath. Again, the Israelites had given their sons and daughters in marriage to foreigners. They had taken their eyes off God while Nehemiah was in Babylon.

Nehemiah swiftly corrected the situations. He removed Tobiah from the temple, reestablished the tithe, and set the Levites back in place to care for the Lord's house. He shut the gates on the Sabbath and called them to remember their covenant to God. Nehemiah prayed for the Lord to look favorably upon him for his efforts to bring reform to the hearts of God's people.

Lord, help us keep our eyes on You. We don't want to become distracted and miss any opportunity to be who You have created us to be.

Job Declares Everything Belongs to God

Then Job arose, and rent his mantle, and shaved his head,
and fell down upon the ground, and worshipped, and said,
Naked came I out of my mother's womb, and naked shall I
return thither: the LORD gave, and the LORD hath taken
away; blessed be the name of the LORD. In all this
Job sinned not, nor charged God foolishly.
JOB 1:20–22

Job, a wealthy man of integrity with a great love for God, was tested. Satan told God that Job served him only because of all the blessings God had given him. So God allowed Job's faith to be tested, and Satan destroyed all he had. His possessions, his servants, and his children were all gone in one day.

Job did not hide his grief but shared his broken heart. Yet in all he said in response to his suffering, the Bible says he did not sin. He continued to love God for who He is and not for what He had given him. Job was uncertain as to why God would allow such terrible things to happen to him, but he declared that everything belongs to God and is His to give and to take.

God, sometimes it is difficult to understand why bad things
happen to people who serve You and do good. Strengthen us
in our faith, and help us build a strong foundation
so we may withstand any test life brings.

Job's Honest Expressions to God

What is man, that thou shouldest magnify him? and that thou
shouldest set thine heart upon him? And that thou shouldest
visit him every morning, and try him every moment?
How long wilt thou not depart from me, nor let me
alone till I swallow down my spittle?

JOB 7:17–19

Job's trust in God demonstrated a close relationship with Him. Most are only transparent with those they know and trust. Job refused to put on a mask and pretend he was okay. Instead, he spoke the reality of his deep hurt and asked God questions that sometimes others might be afraid to ask.

It is likely that Job felt that God had stepped outside of their relationship. Even though he had lived his life obedient to God's will, tragedy happened. He knew he had not sinned, as his friends had suggested for the reason of his situation. He sought assurance that God was still with him in the midst of his grief and would be compassionate toward him once again.

Like Job, you can talk to God as a trusted friend who loves you and has compassion for you. Even when the situations you face in life might try to tell you otherwise, God is on your side.

God, when our emotions are close to eruption, we will speak
with You and talk it out. Give us courage and wisdom
to have honest conversations with You so we might
see things from Your perspective.

Job Asks, "What Is My Purpose?"

Wherefore then hast thou brought me forth out of the womb?
Oh that I had given up the ghost, and no eye had seen me!
I should have been as though I had not been; I should
have been carried from the womb to the grave.
JOB 10:18–19

In the middle of the worst experience in Job's entire life, he questioned his purpose—why was I born? The pain of Job's situation felt unbearable. His desire to live waned. He struggled to see past the terrible things that had happened to him.

Job's tragedy and loss were incomprehensible to most people. He wanted to know what he had done to deserve this horrible situation. His grief deceived him into thinking that God was out to get him (Job 10:13–14, 17). Although God allowed it, Satan had brought this test to him. Job couldn't see it yet, but God was still on his side.

Through all Job endured, he remained faithful to God. He endured great loss and ridicule from his friends. Even his wife told him to curse God and die. But he held on to a small amount of hope that God knew what was best and that his life still held some purpose—even though he didn't know it.

Lord, we will have difficulties in this life. When we face loss,
pain, and hurt, help us remember that we have a purpose.
We were born for such a time as this, and You will
carry us through and restore us.

Job Waits for God's Answers

If a man die, shall he live again? all the days of my
appointed time will I wait, till my change come.
JOB 14:14

Satan attacked Job's motives—the *why* in his decision to serve God. He knew many served God as long as things were good but then deny Him when things become difficult. He accused Job of serving God because God had blessed him with much, not because he loved God.

Satan was not successful in his attempt to break Job's relationship with God through the tests he brought to him. No matter what he put Job through, he was unable to get Job to believe that God—the God he loved and trusted—was not good and just. In all of his expressions of grief, Job never gave up on God. He asked God many questions and tried desperately to understand the *why* while he waited to hear God's reply.

True believers, like Job, find their faith strengthened during adversity. Faith grows as the faithful dig deeper into their relationship with God and hold fast to Him to see Him bring them through to the other side of whatever opposes their faith.

Father God, when our faith is tested, help us hold on to You.
Give us courage to wait on You for the answers we think
we need. Putting our hope and trust in You is the only
way we can experience true victory.

Job's Prayer of Repentance

*Hear, I beseech thee, and I will speak: I will demand of thee,
and declare thou unto me. I have heard of thee by the hearing
of the ear: but now mine eye seeth thee. Wherefore I
abhor myself, and repent in dust and ashes.*
Job 42:4–6

God finally answered Job's many questions with love and compassion. When Job had the opportunity to plead his case, he no longer felt the need to do so. God's answer showed Job that God's actions did not depend on what people do or don't do, but on what He finds necessary to accomplish His plans on the earth.

What Job knew in his heart to be true was once again revealed in God's response. Job's faith was affirmed as he acknowledged that God is omniscient, all-powerful, and wise. His walk of faith revealed that it is more important to know God than to know the answers.

Job's story was far from over. The Lord made Job prosperous again, giving him twice as much as he had before (Job 42:10). The Lord blessed the last part of Job's life more than the first part of his life. God increased his sheep, cattle, oxen, and donkeys. Job had seven more sons and three more daughters and lived a long and full life.

*God, You are the answer. When we don't have the answers,
we choose to trust You anyway. We build our faith on the sure
foundation of Your Word, Your love, and Your compassion.*

David Runs to God

*Arise, O LORD; save me, O my God: for thou hast smitten
all mine enemies upon the cheek bone; thou hast broken the
teeth of the ungodly. Salvation belongeth unto the LORD:
thy blessing is upon thy people.*
PSALM 3:7–8

By the time King David wrote Psalm 3, he may have become used
to people underestimating him. His own father, Jesse, left him
in the field when the prophet Samuel came to anoint the next
king of Israel. Jesse didn't consider him king material even though
God chose him. His oldest brother, Eliab, criticized him when
he asked about the Philistines' champion—the giant Goliath. Yet
David took the giant down with a stone and a sling.

David learned at a young age that it was not his own strength
or charisma that allowed him to accomplish his great lifetime
achievements. He knew that God alone made him the man he was.

David could have sat on his throne and ordered his army to
defend him when his rebellious son, Absalom and the traitors to
David's throne who followed him, rose up against David. Instead,
he fled the palace and ran to God for protection and peace. Instead
of listening to the voices of those around Him, he declared God's
faithfulness. He confidently trusted God to deliver him once again.

*Lord, when situations arise and it seems the world is against us,
we will remember Your faithfulness. We will remind ourselves
of the many times You delivered us. We run to You,
trusting You to do it again.*

David's Prayer Shows Confidence in God

*Hear me when I call, O God of my righteousness: thou hast enlarged
me when I was in distress; have mercy upon me, and hear my prayer.
O ye sons of men, how long will ye turn my glory into shame?
how long will ye love vanity, and seek after leasing? Selah.
But know that the LORD hath set apart him that is godly
for himself: the LORD will hear when I call unto him.*

PSALM 4:1–3

David learned to live dependent on God. It seems he had no one
else to depend on, so at an early age he chose God, who proved
His faithfulness to David many times over. In the times he was
tempted to think God wasn't listening, he probably looked back on
those many times when God faithfully pulled him through sticky
situations to build his faith.

Every believer has seasons when he or she feels alone and
unheard. David refused to believe the lies that he had fallen too far
for God to hear his cry for help. God always delivered—maybe not
the way David expected—but he knew he could count on God to
come through.

As David was pursued by his enemies, he rejoiced in knowing
he was not alone. He trusted that God was with him, heard his
prayers, and would answer him.

*Lord, we build our faith today as we recount the many times
You have proven faithful in our lives. Thank You for always
being there, for always hearing us. Even when we don't
feel Your presence, we know You are with us.*

David's Request for Mercy and Healing

Have mercy upon me, O LORD; for I am weak: O LORD, heal me;
for my bones are vexed. My soul is also sore vexed: but thou,
O LORD, how long? Return, O LORD, deliver my soul:
oh save me for thy mercies' sake.
PSALM 6:2–4

David is often referred to as a man after God's own heart. Acts 13:22 in *The Message* calls him one whose heart beats to the same rhythm as God's. David longed for the things that God wanted. A heart like that would mean David had to be sensitive to the things of God and held a deep desire to please God. Such an intimacy would cause a person to pay attention to the things God is doing and desire to get involved in them.

Although he was not without sin, David had his priorities right. This psalm could have been one of those moments in his life when he recognized he sinned and needed mercy and healing. David came to God with his heart wide open. He knew God could see every single imperfection, and he willingly opened himself up to God's instruction and direction. Through repentance and a willingness to obey, David's expectations were high. He believed he would receive what he asked from his Lord and God!

Our God, we open our hearts before You. Correct and instruct
us. Give us courage to accept what we need to change.
We receive Your mercy and trust You for healing!

David Prays for Refuge and Protection

*I have called upon thee, for thou wilt hear me, O God: incline thine ear
unto me, and hear my speech. Shew thy marvellous lovingkindness,
O thou that savest by thy right hand them which put their trust
in thee from those that rise up against them.*

PSALM 17:6–7

A warrior for God, David began his training as a teenager defending
his father's flock of sheep from predators. He learned at a young age
to depend on God for the battles he faced. With a fierce trust in
God, David stood fearless against a giant champion that dared to
mock his God and took him down with a sling and a stone. The
battles David fought won him honor and praise from the people
and a place in King Saul's army. When the king became jealous of
the admiration David received, he became his enemy as well.

There are many times in David's life when he was running
from an enemy. Often he called on God to protect him from those
who desired to end his life. At one point, King Saul stood just
outside the cave where David hid. David easily could have taken
Saul's life, but he refused to touch God's anointed. Instead, he
relied on God to keep him safe.

*God, You are our hiding place, our safety and security.
When enemies pursue us, we count on You to provide a
way of escape. You always have the answers we need.*

David's Eternal Perspective

*Surely every man walketh in a vain shew: surely they are
disquieted in vain: he heapeth up riches, and knoweth
not who shall gather them. And now, Lord,
what wait I for? my hope is in thee.*
PSALM 39:6–7

As people get older, they reflect on life and recount the things that
mattered. Often the things that seemed very important at the time
pale in comparison to the big picture. In Psalm 39, David explored
just how short life really is. David looked back and lamented how
each person is born with a purpose, yet often the most important
of all things—God's purpose—is left with little done because the
person's focus wasn't on the things that last.

David realized that acquiring daily tasks and building
wealth and treasure on earth make no difference from a heavenly
perspective. David knew that hope for the future rests completely
with the Lord.

David's prayer in Psalm 39 is a revelation that life apart from
God is passing and unfilled. He asked for God's mercy because he
understood that life is short and he perhaps could have done more.
The reality is the things that should receive the most attention are
those things that are important to God.

*God, we want our lives to count long term. Give us strength
to see more than what is directly in front of us. We want to
make a difference that will carry into eternity.*

David's Prayer for the Weak

*Blessed is he that considereth the poor: the LORD will deliver him
in time of trouble. The LORD will preserve him, and keep him alive;
and he shall be blessed upon the earth: and thou wilt not deliver
him unto the will of his enemies. The LORD will strengthen
him upon the bed of languishing: thou
wilt make all his bed in his sickness.*
PSALM 41:1–3

Psalm 41 is one of many places where the Bible addresses God's great care and concern for the poor, weak, and frail. David knew very well what it meant to be weak and understood how important it was to have God's protection in a weak or frail state. As a shepherd boy, he learned very quickly to protect the young, slow, weak, frail, or sick. Any sheep in that condition became the perfect target for predators. As a warrior, David also saw this play out in battle. The enemy looked for the weakest place in an army's defense to gain a foothold.

In Psalm 41, David prayed for himself and for all who are weak. His prayer speaks of physical and emotional weakness, but there is also great risk when someone is spiritually weak. David called on God for mercy and blessing—mercy for his condition and blessing for all who have concern for the weak.

*Heavenly Father, give us hearts of compassion for the weak.
Cover us with Your protection and provision when we are weak.
Give us the courage to stand in faith against those who oppose us.*

A Man's Desire to Thirst for God

O my God, my soul is cast down within me: therefore will I remember
thee from the land of Jordan, and of the Hermonites, from the hill
Mizar. Deep calleth unto deep at the noise of thy waterspouts:
all thy waves and thy billows are gone over me.

PSALM 42:6–7

A downcast soul could be a very good description of depression.
The writer of this psalm was discouraged and distraught, perhaps
feeling separated from God and desperately alone. He was honest
with God about how he felt and expressed his thirst for the presence of God. He needed God's presence as much as a deer needs
water.

The psalmist found the answer for his hurt, pain, and
brokenness in God. He said that he was looking to God to sustain
his very life. He reminded himself of the goodness of God and
how it refreshed his spirit like the roar of waterfalls pouring down.
Through his prayer, he pressed into God for everything he needed.
He closed the psalm with words that expressed his faith and gave
him peace: "Yet the LORD will command his lovingkindness in the
day time, and in the night his song shall be with me, and my prayer
unto the God of my life" (Psalm 42:8).

Lord, we meditate on Your words. We look to You for
encouragement and hope. You are our very life. We recall the
many times You have saved us. Lift our souls into
Your presence, and restore us today.

David Trusts God for Everything

I will freely sacrifice unto thee: I will praise thy name, O LORD;
for it is good. For he hath delivered me out of all trouble:
and mine eye hath seen his desire upon mine enemies.
PSALM 54:6–7

David spent a lot of time running from ruthless men who wanted to destroy him in one way or another. Some were enemies from far-off lands, some were his own people and his own family. His psalms often ebb and flow, beginning with the brutal truth of where he was emotionally and the reality of the challenge he faced that needed God's intervention, followed by words of his faith-filled expectation of what God would do on his behalf.

David relied on God to save him from whomever and whatever chased after him. Those who looked at David saw him for who he was on the outside—a shepherd, musician, poet, soldier, and king. David's perception of himself—for the most part—was as a man who could do nothing in his own ability but was mighty only through his dependence on God. In Psalm 54, David called on God to overcome his enemies and help him in the face of hurt and betrayal.

Lord, we are nothing without You. We endeavor to be honest
with who we are and how we feel. We want to know
more of who You are. We trust You to keep us from
harm and save us from our enemies.

David Prays While Overwhelmed by Fear

As for me, I will call upon God; and the LORD shall save me.
Evening, and morning, and at noon, will I pray, and cry aloud:
and he shall hear my voice. He hath delivered my soul
in peace from the battle that was against me:
for there were many with me.
PSALM 55:16–18

David wrote this psalm likely during his son Absalom's rebellion and Ahithophel's betrayal. Absalom conspired against his father to overthrow him and take over the throne. Ahithophel, once David's friend and adviser, joined Absalom and betrayed David, his king.

David prayed, "My heart is sore pained within me: and the terrors of death are fallen upon me" (Psalm 55:4). He was standing in the midst of dark, deep fear and the pain from the fact that those he loved so much had turned against him and wanted to kill him.

There is little that hurts more than for someone close to you—friend or family—to betray you. David called on God morning, noon, and night and reminded himself (and God) of the times God saved him. He remembered how God heard him and would save him once again.

God, You alone can heal the wounds we have suffered at
the hands of those we loved and trusted. Touch our hearts
and heal our wounds. Give us faith to stand and believe that
You will save us and turn difficult situations for our good.

David Asks God to Be His Shelter

Hear my cry, O God; attend unto my prayer. From the end of the earth will I cry unto thee, when my heart is overwhelmed: lead me to the rock that is higher than I. For thou hast been a shelter for me, and a strong tower from the enemy. I will abide in thy tabernacle for ever: I will trust in the covert of thy wings.

PSALM 61:1–4

David may have been far from home, alone and looking for refuge. No matter how many times in his life he felt lost and alone, he was *never* alone. God was always with him, and he knew it. He trusted God to be with him no matter where his journey took him.

God provided for David physically and spiritually. David may have needed shelter in nature and looked to God to show him a safe place where he would rest. But God was also David's safe haven that sheltered him from all the emotional and mental challenges. Even though David asked for forgiveness and God forgave him for his sins, there were consequences for his actions.

Like many of us today, David could have had a list of "if onlys" that scrolled through his head when things were difficult. Instead of getting lost in those moments, perhaps he prayed and allowed God to become his refuge from those times in his life as well.

God, You are more than enough for anything that concerns us. We call on You, and You answer us. Be our strong tower and refuge today.

David's Swan Song

Thou makest the outgoings of the morning and evening to rejoice.
Thou visitest the earth, and waterest it: . . .thou preparest them corn,
when thou hast so provided for it. Thou waterest the ridges thereof
abundantly: thou settlest the furrows thereof: thou makest it soft
with showers: thou blessest the springing thereof.
PSALM 65:8–10

King David is known for both his infamous sins and his God-directed heart. He was a sinner who always returned his heart to God. He was a warrior and a poet. His life often seemed a great contradiction.

This prayer song was written toward the end of David's life. He could have reflected on the betrayal of his son Absalom, the injustice of King Saul, or the personal sins he knew all too well. Instead, David came to the end of his life with a heart of praise to the God who forgives.

Solomon was David's son who would become king after his death. Solomon, at the end of his life, would write Ecclesiastes. This book paints a rather depressing picture of a king who was given every advantage and failed to remember that all gifts come from a good God. "Therefore I hated life; because the work that is wrought under the sun is grievous unto me: for all is vanity and vexation of spirit" (2:17).

The end of our life is a powerful testimony to the decisions we have made. We may be like David and recount the wonder of a creative and loving God; or we might be like Solomon who had trouble understanding that life really does have meaning.

Finish well.

Father, when we come to the end of our life, may we have lived in
such a way that we can hear You say, "Well done, good and faithful
servant! Come and share your Master's happiness!"

Praise for God's Power, Favor, and Goodness

For thou, O God, hast proved us: thou hast tried us, as silver is tried.
Thou broughtest us into the net; thou laidst affliction upon our loins.
Thou hast caused men to ride over our heads; we went through
fire and through water: but thou broughtest us out into a wealthy
place. I will go into thy house with burnt offerings: I will pay
thee my vows, which my lips have uttered, and my mouth
hath spoken, when I was in trouble.
PSALM 66:10–14

In medieval culture there were damsels, knights, kings, queens, jesters, and bards.

A bard used poetic song to share infamous battles and the feats of the brave. Listeners would thrill to tales of chivalry, infamy, and history.

Perhaps the bards learned early the words of Psalm 66. This prayer song tells of the God who was close enough to hear and strong enough to act. The song recounted God's faithfulness. The words energized while inviting listeners to praise.

This history song was filled with honor, as well as the pain of struggle. Praise always came before and after the darkest moments. "Make a joyful noise unto God, all ye lands: Sing forth the honour of his name: make his praise glorious. . . . All the earth shall worship thee, and shall sing unto thee; they shall sing to thy name" (Psalm 66:1–2, 4).

We are left crying to God for mercy and praising Him for relief. When your mind connects with this song, you will discover that the same God who moved the psalmist to write these words is the same God you have access to today.

Father, we are grateful that when Jesus died on the cross,
the curtain that separated us from Your Most Holy Place was
torn from top to bottom, so that we might confidently
enter into Your presence at any time.

David Passes the Torch

*Give the king thy judgments, O God, and thy righteousness
unto the king's son. He shall judge thy people with
righteousness, and thy poor with judgment.*
PSALM 72:1–2

❧ ❧

Many kings in the Bible were booted off their thrones by power-hungry sons or those whose job it was to protect the king. Few kings named their replacements because their successors would often end their lives first.

King David was clear about who would succeed him as king. Psalm 72 is a prayer that may have been part of Solomon's inauguration: "He shall judge the poor of the people, he shall save the children of the needy, and shall break in pieces the oppressor. They shall fear thee as long as the sun and moon endure, throughout all generations" (Psalm 72:4–5).

In a perfect world, you would expect a loving father to bless his son in the work he has been given to do, but in giving up your throne so your son could rule, there must have been a unique sense that God would equip the young man to lead. God came through. He gave Solomon wisdom that surpassed any other. Like his father, Solomon had moments of failure. Like his father, Solomon led the people in understanding and following God.

David's prayer ended perfectly with a reminder of who they were really celebrating that day: "Blessed be the LORD God, the God of Israel, who only doeth wondrous things. And blessed be his glorious name for ever: and let the whole earth be filled with his glory; Amen, and Amen" (verses 18–19).

*Praise be to You, Lord of heaven and earth. You depose kings
and raise up others. Raise up godly leaders for us, O Lord.*

Hopeful Prayer of a Sinful Man

Behold, O God our shield, and look upon the face of thine anointed.
For a day in thy courts is better than a thousand. I had rather be
a doorkeeper in the house of my God, than to dwell in the tents
of wickedness. For the LORD God is a sun and shield: the LORD
will give grace and glory: no good thing will he withhold
from them that walk uprightly.

PSALM 84:9–11

Maybe you have sung these words from Psalm 84 in a church service and come away feeling like it is a pretty wonderful thing to spend a little time with God. The New Testament's prodigal son would have understood this idea very well. After essentially throwing away his inheritance, he went home. When he saw his dad, he said, "I will arise and go to my father, and will say unto him, Father, I have sinned against heaven, and before thee, and am no more worthy to be called thy son: make me as one of thy hired servants" (Luke 15:18–19).

Why would the prodigal son understand this psalm more than most? The writer of this prayer was relaying the hope of a sinful man. He was really saying something like, "I am unworthy to ask, but spending one day in Your court as the lowliest of servants would be better than living years away from You. If I could just grovel at the threshold of Your temple, I'd consider this the greatest work I could do with my broken life."

That is the similarity between this psalmist and the prodigal son. They proclaim their unworthiness to one who overwhelmingly loves and accepts them.

When we understand God's greatness, we can fully appreciate His love.

Thank You, gracious Father, for making Your children
to be a kingdom of priests to serve You in this life
and in the life to come. We have no higher calling.

David's Good Struggle

Be merciful unto me, O Lord: for I cry unto thee daily.
Rejoice the soul of thy servant: for unto thee, O Lord, do I lift
up my soul. For thou, Lord, art good, and ready to forgive;
and plenteous in mercy unto all them that call upon thee.
Psalm 86:3–5

Psalm 86 is a prayer of King David. Read virtually any chapter on his life and you will see the opposition he faced. From Goliath to King Saul. From his brothers to his sons.

David struggled with outside pressures as well as the flawed inner man he could never change on his own. His prayers and psalms come from a place that either caught a pure glimpse of God or a position that fixates on the struggles he faced.

Imagine those two places wrestling for expression in his prayers. Psalm 86 provides a sample of that prayer. On one hand, David prayed, "Rejoice the soul of thy servant" (verse 4). He admitted he needed help. The prayer continues, "Thou, Lord, art good, and ready to forgive" (verse 5).

This pattern is repeated often in this prayer: I'm struggling, but You are good.

"Teach me thy way, O Lord. . .I will praise thee" (verses 11–12).

"Violent men have sought after my soul. . . .Thou, O Lord, art a God full of compassion" (verses 14–15).

"Shew me a token for good. . .thou, Lord, hast holpen me, and comforted me" (verse 17).

For every struggle we face, we have an opportunity to praise an awesome God. Share your pain with God. He can take it. Don't stop there. Honor Him in your struggle.

Lord, You are a merciful God who takes no pleasure in our pain.
Use our trials to make us strong as we walk by faith and not by sight.

Prayer of a Troubled Soul

*O lord God of my salvation, I have cried day and night before
thee: . . .incline thine ear unto my cry; for my soul is full of
troubles. . . I am counted with them that go down into
the pit: I am as a man that hath no strength.*
PSALM 88:1–4

We don't need to know the author of this psalm to relate to the deep
feelings of pain expressed throughout the God-directed prayer.

This prayer expresses feelings of rejection, abandonment,
anger, physical illness, and the desperation of a man who feels like
he is drowning spiritually.

Unlike the majority of prayers, this one does not include praise.
It is lonely and bitter, and there are never words of apology for
feeling this way. "LORD, why castest thou off my soul? why hidest
thou thy face from me?" (Psalm 88:14).

If you think this prayer is for those of us who struggle with
admitting we've felt this way, you are partially right. This prayer
may be better understood by thinking of the final days of Jesus' life.

Some might say that portions of this prayer were speaking
prophetically of a time when Jesus would be betrayed and God
would turn His back on the sin His Son carried for us.

Those who read the scriptures would have been able to recall
this prayer, and when they did, they might just see Jesus in the
midst of the pain expressed here.

No matter what you have endured, you have access to a Savior
who fully understands rejection, abandonment, anger, physical
illness, and desperation.

*Lord Jesus, we take comfort in knowing that You experienced
every sort of trial we experience. And we are grateful that
You overcame those trials by Your death and resurrection
so that we might be empowered to be overcomers, too.*

Moses' Important Admission

So teach us to number our days, that we may apply our hearts unto wisdom. Return, O Lord, how long? and let it repent thee concerning thy servants. . . . And let the beauty of the Lord our God be upon us: and establish thou the work of our hands upon us; yea, the work of our hands establish thou it.
PSALM 90:12–13, 17

The first humans were made of the dust of the earth. We're fragile and described as grass that withers or disappearing water vapor or smoke. After death our bodies return to dust.

Our entire existence is sustained by God. Our hope rests in His favor.

In contrast, God is eternal. He always was and always will be. He is never worried about an end to His existence. He has never needed to set His affairs in order. He only had one birth announcement to make. Instead of cards, God sent angels.

Moses was only too aware that mankind faced limitations that God didn't face. In this prayer, Moses expressed the majesty of God and frailty of man. This is why a prayer that asked God to establish the works of his hands was an important admission. This prayer acknowledged God's goodness and man's need: "Satisfy us early with thy mercy; that we may rejoice and be glad all our days" (Psalm 90:14).

Life can be difficult to endure. We suffer pain, endure heartache, and look for purpose. Like Moses, we can honor God, seek His plan for our lives, and learn from the One who created with words. Our choices about God will always have more meaning than what we include on our bucket list.

Father, remind us daily to make the most of every precious moment You give us on this earth. May we glorify You in our every act.

A Prayer of Trust

My days are like a shadow that declineth; and I am withered
like grass. But thou, O LORD, shall endure for ever;
and thy remembrance unto all generations.
PSALM 102:11–12

The writer of this prayer recognized that his days were coming to an end. He also understood affliction but knew that God always comes through.

Passing along a message to future generations was important to the writer. God doesn't overlook those who struggle. He doesn't close His eyes, block His ears, and harden His heart. Even if this writer never saw further evidence of God's faithfulness, he could still conclude that his grandchildren's grandchildren needed to know that God loves them deeply.

Fully understanding that the pain the writer endured was not hypothetical is key. Instead of spending a lot of time wondering why God allowed pain, this psalmist wanted a new generation to understand that no matter what you go through, God can always be trusted with the result.

Loving Father, because You have promised eternal life to
those who trust in the work of Your Son on the cross, we do not
need to fear death when our bodies start to grow weak.
Thank You for this great hope.

An Expression of Praise

Praise ye the LORD. O give thanks unto the LORD;
for he is good: for his mercy endureth for ever.
PSALM 106:1

The opening lines to Psalm 106 are essential to understanding what follows. Read each remaining line to find reminders of some of the most painful times in the history of national sin. Although we may conclude that there is negativity in the heart of the psalmist, this may be an incorrect assumption.

The opening lines speak of God's goodness and invite all to join in collective gratitude. Why follow this expression of praise with negative word pictures and historical moments many would have been happy to forget? Each reminder points to the poor decisions of man and the goodness of a sin-intolerant God: "Save us, O LORD our God, and gather us from among the heathen, to give thanks unto thy holy name, and to triumph in thy praise" (verse 47).

This prayer reminds us that no matter how good our intentions may be, no matter how hard we try, and no matter what excuses we come up with, we will make mistakes. And we will need a good God to rescue us.

There is no sugarcoating in this prayer. It brings up what may have been stinging memories or may have reminded the people of the worst part of the "good old days." Perhaps this was important so the hearer would be less inclined to seek glory that could belong only to the God who saves.

Jesus, You warned us that in this world we would have trouble.
But You also tell us to take heart because You have overcome
the world. No matter how tough times may get,
we can rejoice that You are in control.

David's Yearning for Justice

They compassed me about also with words of hatred;
and fought against me without a cause. For my love they
are my adversaries: but I give myself unto prayer. And they have
rewarded me evil for good, and hatred for my love.
PSALM 109:3–5

In the New Testament, Jesus said we should love those who don't return the favor. It is better to be repaid by God than by the person to whom we show kindness. However, that doesn't prevent our own prayers of lamentation when we are misunderstood, misused, and mistreated.

David prayed just this kind of prayer in Psalm 109. He wasn't passing along intel to a divine leader. God already knew. David was pouring out a heart that yearned for justice. He was angry.

As the psalm unfolds, we find that David had man-centered plans for his enemy that included a guilty verdict, the loss of family, bankruptcy, persecution, and a broken heart. David didn't like this guy.

God listened, but if He had agreed to what David wanted, He would have violated His own law.

Perhaps this psalm is profound proof that God doesn't condemn us for being uncharitable in our personal prayers. The act of praying what is really on our heart tends to bring us to a place of calm assurance that God has our hardest moments under His control. More than changing others, God wants to change us, and we are so much better for His compassionate transformation.

Jesus, You gave us instructions that are impossible to follow
in our own power. You said that we must love our enemies
and even pray for them. Please fill us with your life-
transforming love so that we can do what You command.

David's Prayer Aroma

Lord, I cry unto thee: make haste unto me; give ear unto
my voice, when I cry unto thee. Let my prayer be set forth
before thee as incense; and the lifting up of my
hands as the evening sacrifice.
PSALM 141:1–2

If our attitude has an odor, then some people enter a room with the same attention-grabbing result of an angry skunk while others arrive with the pleasing aroma of your favorite spices. The difference is undeniable.

David's prayer is described in just such a way. He wanted to extend his prayer as a pleasing aroma to God, because David wanted to spend time fully focused on the object of his worship.

Perhaps David could remember personal prayers that didn't always have a pleasing aroma. Perhaps he thought of the many times he allowed his humanity to dictate his response. Perhaps he remembered the God who patiently endured.

Because David had been up close and personal with bad behavior in others, this prayer can be seen as a request for protection against living down to their example. "Set a watch, O LORD, before my mouth; keep the door of my lips. Incline not my heart to any evil thing, to practise wicked works with men that work iniquity: and let me not eat of their dainties" (Psalm 141:3–4).

To humbly request that God keep us from sinful patterns of behavior must have a pleasing aroma to a trustworthy God.

Father, Your Word says that we are to You the pleasing
aroma of Christ among those who are being saved and
those who are perishing. Use us to spread the aroma
of the knowledge of Christ everywhere.

David's Prayer for Refuge

*I cried unto the LORD with my voice; with my voice unto the LORD
did I make my supplication. I poured out my complaint before
him; I shewed before him my trouble. When my spirit
was overwhelmed within me, then thou knewest my path.*

PSALM 142:1–3

David had fled the comforts of home. He and his companions had
sought shelter in a cave, waiting for King Saul to end his pursuit
and go home.

David had been anointed king of Israel. Saul, the current king,
was aware that David was to be king, but two thoughts prevented
him from giving up his throne: (1) Saul liked being king, and (2)
he wanted his own son to rule when he died. For Saul, the only
reasonable plan of action was to kill David. If he were dead, then
he couldn't be king.

This prayer was written with those thoughts swirling through
the mind of David. The cold, echoing chamber of the cave was the
place where he would say, "Attend unto my cry; for I am brought
very low: deliver me from my persecutors; for they are stronger
than I" (Psalm 142:6).

We can often find ourselves way outside our comfort zone. In
this place of uncertainty, we may have an unexpected appointment
with God. His glory always shows up when we admit we can't
manage on our own. His help is always invited on bended knee.
His love is ours before we are wise enough to call on His name.

*Father, when we are in trouble and call on Your name,
You promise to answer us, be with us, and deliver us.
What more could we ask!*

David's God-Esteem

*Deliver me, O LORD, from mine enemies: I flee unto thee to
hide me. Teach me to do thy will; for thou art my God:
thy spirit is good; lead me into the land of uprightness.*

PSALM 143:9-10

Have you ever felt so frustrated by life that you think, *God I need
Your help, Your wisdom, Your strength, and Your hope; I can't make it
through this day without You?*

God is aware that we can't manage every crisis on our own,
which is why He is everything we need. He can be trusted with
both justice and grace. He is *God*. Nothing escapes His attention.

David penned this prayer. Unwrap the layers, and you will find
two truths: God is good, and I am not.

In David's prayer, we can see that he felt inadequate because he
sinned, his enemy was stronger, he didn't have answers, his life was in
danger, and there was no place other than God where he didn't face
trouble. Life was out of his control.

David demonstrated God-esteem instead of self-esteem. He
could count all the ways he failed and needed help, but there was
nothing about God that was inferior. He cried out, "Cause me to
hear thy lovingkindness in the morning; for in thee do I trust: cause
me to know the way wherein I should walk; for I lift up my soul
unto thee" (Psalm 143:8).

God-esteem prevents us from looking at life as something we
can use to prove we don't need God, and instead as something that
God can use to perform everyday miracles through regular people—like us.

*Father, You are God and we are not. But remind us always
that You have raised us up with Christ and seated us with
Him in the heavenly realms in order that in the coming
ages You might show the incomparable riches of Your
grace, expressed in Your kindness to us in Your Son.*

Jeremiah's Loss for Words

Then said I, Ah, Lord God! behold,
I cannot speak: for I am a child.
JEREMIAH 1:6

We don't know exactly how old Jeremiah was when he had this conversation with God. What we know is that God gave him a job, and when God employs, He also equips. Jeremiah may not have realized that he could do what God wanted him to do, but the fact remains that God gave him the job of a prophet, and Jeremiah was ready whether he felt like it or not.

To reassure the young man, the Lord replied, "Say not, I am a child: for thou shalt go to all that I shall send thee, and whatsoever I command thee thou shalt speak. Be not afraid of their faces: for I am with thee to deliver thee" (Jeremiah 1:7–8).

What stood between God's will and Jeremiah's willingness was a little thing called *obedience*. To remove any stumbling block for the young prophet, God answered questions Jeremiah hadn't even thought to ask. God promised to give him the words to say, the courage to stand up to dignitaries, and to watch over everything Jeremiah would do, and He would give Jeremiah His personal protection.

Life would not be easy for the prophet, and there would be times he wished he didn't have the responsibility of speaking for God, but he was given words to say that came from the heart of God.

Jeremiah obeyed.

Heavenly Father, thank You for the examples of people in Your Word who obeyed You even though doing so meant hardship. We think of Noah, Abraham, Moses, Daniel, and others who changed the world by obeying You. May we follow in their steps.

Jeremiah's Coming Correction

O Lord, I know that the way of man is not in himself:
it is not in man that walketh to direct his steps. O Lord,
correct me, but with judgment; not in thine anger,
lest thou bring me to nothing.
JEREMIAH 10:23–24

When parents discipline a child in anger, they often go too far and regret their decisions, and tension develops between child and parent for a while. At the time of this prayer, Jeremiah had followed God's command to be His prophet. He acknowledged that the people needed God's direction to make decisions. When it came to discipline, Jeremiah asked that God correct only when He wasn't angry. Jeremiah understood that standing before an angry God could lead to destruction.

God's people were making sinful choices, and it wasn't unreasonable to understand God's anger as justified. However, Jeremiah had a request: "Pour out thy fury upon the heathen that know thee not, and upon the families that call not on thy name" (Jeremiah 10:25).

It is important to remember that Jeremiah wasn't God. He was not correcting an equal. Jeremiah was simply praying with the knowledge of one specially prepared to speak to others in God's behalf. Jeremiah was responding to God from the perspective of one who had learned much and understood the need for justice. Jeremiah suggested that if wrath was inevitable, perhaps it would be best spent on those who had already chosen to reject God, but Jeremiah didn't know what God knew.

Help us Father to trust that You always have our best interests at heart.
We know that You work in all things for the good of those who love
You, who have been called according to Your purpose.

Jeremiah Questions Justice

Righteous art thou, O LORD, when I plead with thee:
yet let me talk with thee of thy judgments: Wherefore doth
the way of the wicked prosper? wherefore are all they
happy that deal very treacherously?
JEREMIAH 12:1

We have all been around people who think they have gotten away with something. Maybe they didn't report extra income on their tax filings and they have never been caught. Maybe they found a loophole in a law and they are exploiting something that may not be legal. Maybe they took something that belonged to another.

Jeremiah once prayed for his nation. He asked God to consider directing His anger elsewhere, but a growing national evil caused Jeremiah to change his mind and ask God to accelerate justice in this prayer: "How long shall the land mourn, and the herbs of every field wither, for the wickedness of them that dwell therein? the beasts are consumed, and the birds; because they said, He shall not see our last end" (Jeremiah 12:4).

When God answered Jeremiah, it was to let him know in very specific terms that justice was on the way and it would be painful, but that justice would ultimately lead the people to turn away from sin. There would even come a day when God would restore what was lost in the time of justice, but only to those nations who returned to Him.

There is always a price to pay when broken people insist on rebellion.

Jesus, You taught us to guard against hypocrisy and warned
that there is nothing concealed that will not be disclosed.
You said that what we say in the dark will be heard in
the daylight and what we say in secret will be proclaimed
from the rooftops. Keep us, Lord, from such evil.

Jeremiah. . .Prayer of the Weeping Prophet

*Behold the mounts, they are come unto the city to take it; and the city
is given into the hand of the Chaldeans, that fight against it,
because of the sword, and of the famine, and of the pestilence:
and what thou hast spoken is come to pass; and, behold, thou seest it.*
JEREMIAH 32:24

God used Jeremiah to warn the people of Israel that they would be
removed from the land due to unconstrained national sin. Jeremiah
has been called the "weeping prophet." His tears were for the soon
vanquished nation as well as for the compulsion to deliver the
message God had given him.

The Babylonians settled in to attack Jerusalem, yet God
instructed Jeremiah to do something strange, considering the
circumstances. He told Jeremiah to purchase a piece of land. It
would be decades before Jerusalem would be rebuilt under the
leadership of Nehemiah, yet the purchase of land was a very clear
illustration that God's punishment of the nation would not last
forever. The Jewish people would return home, and there would
once more be property to own, crops to tend, and herds to care for.

Although imprisoned for sharing an unpopular message from
God, Jeremiah was able to pray, "Ah Lord God! behold, thou hast
made the heaven and the earth by thy great power and stretched out
arm, and there is nothing too hard for thee. . . . Great in counsel,
and mighty in work" (Jeremiah 32:17, 19).

Justice had finally come, but even this correction was only for
a season.

*Loving Father, Your punishment always fits the crime,
for You are just. Thank You for showing us that You love us
by disciplining us when we need to be corrected.*

Jeremiah's Lament Begins

Behold, O LORD; for I am in distress: my bowels are troubled;
mine heart is turned within me; for I have grievously rebelled:
abroad the sword bereaveth, at home there is as death.
LAMENTATIONS 1:20

Jeremiah was very clear in his declaration that Israel would be forsaken, carried off by Babylon and the people scattered. However, this news was distressing for Jeremiah to see after most of the Israelites had been forced to relocate to Babylon.

This prayer comes in the first chapter of the book of tears. These lamentations are the accumulated emotional wailings associated with knowing justice would come and having to endure it.

Jeremiah could see and hear all those who gloated at the downfall of Israel. In brokenness he prayed, "Let all their wickedness come before thee; and do unto them, as thou hast done unto me for all my transgressions: for my sighs are many, and my heart is faint" (Lamentations 1:22).

Jeremiah's message of doom was not one he shared with joy. He was not happy to relate the news that the people had offended a righteous God. He knew the day was coming, but the time of justice left him with a lamentation song, not an inclination to tell the world, "I told you so."

While Jeremiah wept for his people in Babylon, God had already established young Hebrew men there who were righteous, faithful, and committed to prayer. You might remember Daniel.

Father, You will not despise a broken and contrite heart.
Forgive us our trespasses, and restore us to right standing
with You through the blood of Your Son.

Daniel's Prayer for the Nation

*O Lord, the great and dreadful God, keeping the covenant
and mercy to them that love him, and to them that keep his
commandments; we have sinned, and have committed iniquity,
and have done wickedly, and have rebelled, even by departing
from thy precepts and from thy judgments: neither have we
hearkened unto thy servants the prophets, which spake in
thy name to our kings, our princes, and our fathers,
and to all the people of the land.*
DANIEL 9:4–6

Daniel was an early exile to Babylon. While Jeremiah lamented the destruction of Jerusalem, Daniel was reading the prophet's account of the siege. Daniel understood that the exile would last seventy years, and this news caused Daniel to pray earnestly for his nation.

Daniel didn't pray for a reduced sentence. He prayed as one who represented all who had sinned. Even though his life was defined by righteousness, he prayed, "Neither have we obeyed the voice of the LORD our God, to walk in his laws, which he set before us by his servants the prophets. . . . And he hath confirmed his words, which he spake against us, and against our judges that judged us, by bringing upon us a great evil: for under the whole heaven hath not been done as hath been done upon Jerusalem. As it is written in the law of Moses, all this evil is come upon us: yet made we not our prayer before the LORD our God, that we might turn from our iniquities, and understand thy truth" (Daniel 9:10, 12–13).

*Father, we humble ourselves and seek Your face and turn
from our wicked ways. Please hear our prayer for forgiveness,
and heal our land. We ask this in Jesus' name and for His sake.*

Daniel Questions How
It Will Finally End

And I heard, but I understood not: then said I,
O my Lord, what shall be the end of these things?
DANIEL 12:8

Daniel prayed a prayer we can all identify with. His prayer didn't start with "Dear God," and it didn't end with "Amen." Daniel's prayer was based in a curiosity we all can identify with: "How will all this finally end?"

Daniel was being given a prophecy that pertained to the final days of earth. This man had already seen the exile of his home country and had lamented with the rest. Now he was being told about the end of time. What Daniel was told, he wrote down. It is probable he didn't understand everything, but he fully understood that what he heard was important.

We can relate to Daniel, can't we? The end of time is something we all think about from time to time, but we may struggle with understanding what everything means. We look at the world around us and wonder if things can get any worse before Jesus returns. Like Daniel, we can ask, "How will all this finally end?"

Instead of giving Daniel a direct answer, the Lord told him through an angel, "Many shall be purified, and made white, and tried; but the wicked shall do wickedly: and none of the wicked shall understand; but the wise shall understand" (Daniel 12:10).

Daniel was one of the wisest men in Babylon. He knew only God could bring clarity.

Father, no eye has seen, no ear has heard, and no mind has conceived
what You have prepared for those You love, but You reveal
these things to us by Your Spirit. Thank You, Lord!

Sailors' "Man Overboard" Prayer

Wherefore they cried unto the LORD, and said, We beseech thee,
O LORD, we beseech thee, let us not perish for this man's life,
and lay not upon us innocent blood: for thou, O LORD,
hast done as it pleased thee.
JONAH 1:14

Jonah was a prophet of God. He passed along God's messages. Jonah was told to go to Nineveh and tell them it was time to repent.

We may not understand Jonah's dislike of the people of Nineveh, but his feelings suddenly made obedience optional. Apparently Jonah was the only one who thought so. The prophet booked passage on a ship heading in the opposite direction. While Jonah slept, God sent a storm that convinced a bunch of hardened sailors that God was behind the storm. When Jonah confessed that he was running away from God, the sailors added prayer to their newfound respect for God. Their prayer came just before they tossed Jonah overboard and watched a big fish give Jonah a three-day time-out to consider the consequences of disobedience.

While Jonah contemplated decisions from inside the fish, the sailors marveled that the mighty storm went away after Jonah's course took a divine redirection.

God can take something undesirable, like disobedience, and turn it into an opportunity to show others His power, justice, and desire for obedience. If God got this point across to some sailors, just imagine what He would do for those in Nineveh—and a prophet named Jonah.

Father, thank You for taking things that are meant for evil
and turning them into something good. And thank You
for being a God of second chances.

Jonah's Matter of Three Days

*The waters compassed me about, even to the soul: the depth closed
me round about, the weeds were wrapped about my head. . . .
But I will sacrifice unto thee with the voice of thanksgiving;
I will pay that that I have vowed. Salvation is of the LORD.*
JONAH 2:5, 9

For three days Jonah lived inside a fish featuring less than five-star accommodations. He reconsidered his view on optional obedience. He was tired of his personal submarine, seaweed, and water. But his sabbatical inside a fish on the outskirts of Nineveh caused him to sing a song. Obedience was replacing stubborn pride, and he had a renewed willingness to keep the vows of a prophet. "The LORD spake unto the fish, and it vomited out Jonah upon the dry land" (Jonah 2:10).

Jesus Himself would use Jonah's situation to help develop a word picture for His own death. "For as Jonas was three days and three nights in the whale's belly; so shall the Son of man be three days and three nights in the heart of the earth" (Matthew 12:40).

While never surprised at the stubbornness of humanity, Jesus spoke of Jonah because the prophet's message was accepted and acted on after spending time in the belly of a fish. Jesus was God's Son and would willingly spend three days in death, yet the majority of people He came to rescue would choose poor eternal accommodations by rejecting His salvation plan.

*Thank You, Father, for Your wondrous plan for our salvation.
Thank You, Jesus, for tasting death for us and rising from the
dead three days later so that we might dwell in Your presence
in the place You are preparing for us to live forever.*

Jonah's Tantrum

And [Jonah] prayed unto the Lord, and said, I pray thee,
O Lord, was not this my saying, when I was yet in my country?
Therefore I fled before unto Tarshish: for I knew that thou art a
gracious God, and merciful, slow to anger, and of great kindness,
and repentest thee of the evil. Therefore now, O Lord, take,
I beseech thee, my life from me; for it is better for me to die than
to live. Then said the Lord, Doest thou well to be angry?
Jonah 4:2–4

Apparently three days in a fish was enough for Jonah to understand that God wanted him to obey, but it seems he still hoped the people of Nineveh wouldn't listen to his God-sent message. They did, and Jonah was mad. His anger shows in his prayer. He seems to be saying, "I told You something like this would happen. You are way too compassionate. They repent. You forgive. I didn't want to see that happen. Just kill me now." If Jonah's actions come across as an infantile tantrum, it is because they *were* an infantile tantrum.

God asked Jonah a great question: "Is it right for you to be angry?" The question is rhetorical. The answer is no.

As the people of God, we are to embrace compassion, not just for ourselves but for others. If each person got what he or she deserved, then all of us would be doomed. We sin and deserve death, but God's compassion offers forgiveness and restoration. Jonah struggled to accept the truth that God could be compassionate to anyone at any time for any reason.

Father, may we learn to be kind and compassionate to one another,
forgiving each other, just as in Christ, You forgave us.

Habakkuk's Operation: Restorative Justice

O LORD, how long shall I cry, and thou wilt not hear! even cry out unto thee of violence, and thou wilt not save! Why dost thou shew me iniquity, and cause me to behold grievance? for spoiling and violence are before me. . .and judgment doth never go forth: for the wicked doth compass about the righteous; therefore wrong judgment proceedeth.

HABAKKUK 1:2–4

Habakkuk prayed what many have thought. The prophet seems to suggest that the law of the land was a colossal joke. He felt that decisions were made by rule of the wicked. The law was no longer effective. This prayer to God also covered the offenses of evil deeds, destruction, violence, and a seeming lack of divine response.

God's answer provided clarity to Habakkuk's concerns: "I raise up the Chaldeans, that bitter and hasty nation, which shall march through the breadth of the land, to possess the dwellingplaces that are not their's" (Habakkuk 1:6).

There was no mention of God demanding that people play nice and love each other. There was no indication that people would simply realize they were wrong and apologize. God's answer was invasion.

The enemy would be bent on violence, rely on their own strength, capture enemies, and be extremely cruel. This enemy would not be coming to give a seminar on how to be a model citizen. They wouldn't pass out pamphlets on the value of respecting the law. They would arrive to conquer and take by force.

God's answer was far more comprehensive than Habakkuk may have wanted. The options were removed from the plan. The people of Israel would have plenty of time to consider their actions in Babylon. Restorative justice was on its way.

Father, life in our nation today is much like the situation You addressed through Habakkuk. Raise up leaders in Your Church, Lord, that will help us to be the salt and light You have called us to be.

Habakkuk Questions God's Tolerance

Art thou not from everlasting, O LORD my God, mine Holy One?
we shall not die. O LORD, thou hast ordained them for judgment;
and, O mighty God, thou hast established them for correction.
Thou art of purer eyes than to behold evil, and canst not look
on iniquity: wherefore lookest thou upon them that deal
treacherously, and holdest thy tongue when the wicked
devoureth the man that is more righteous than he?
HABAKKUK 1:12–13

Habakkuk was conflicted, knowing the Babylonians would be God's choice for correcting Israel. Babylon was powerful, ruthless, and formidable. Could God really use a nation that didn't honor Him to discipline His people?

God's response made it clear that He was aware of the sin of Babylon, and they would be punished. God had rescued His people from Egypt. He would rescue again. "The LORD answered me, and said, Write the vision, and make it plain upon tables, that he may run that readeth it. For the vision is yet for an appointed time, but at the end it shall speak, and not lie: though it tarry, wait for it; because it will surely come, it will not tarry" (Habakkuk 2:2–3).

Even when the world seems as if it cannot help but get worse, God wants us to know that He has things firmly in control, and if we are patient we will see Him rescue again. If the in-between time seems a little frightening, we should remember that God has never left anything half finished.

We choose to trust in You, Father, rather than fearing the future.
You have prepared us for unfolding events by warning us in
Your Word. Each of the earth's birth pains signals that
we are closer to the time of Your glorious coming.

Habakkuk's Prayer of Praise

*Although the fig tree shall not blossom, neither shall fruit be
in the vines; the labour of the olive shall fail, and the fields
shall yield no meat; the flock shall be cut off from the fold,
and there shall be no herd in the stalls: yet I will rejoice
in the Lord, I will joy in the God of my salvation.*
HABAKKUK 3:17–18

Compassion can lead people to repent, and compassion might have
been the preferred way to transform a rebellious people, but God
was clear. Justice meant exile. This prayer song finds Habakkuk in a
place of acceptance. For the first time, the prophet could pray for a
people who would finally seek God after an extended season of sin.
"O Lord, I have heard thy speech, and was afraid: O Lord, revive
thy work in the midst of the years, in the midst of the years make
known; in wrath remember mercy" (Habakkuk 3:2).

Habakkuk remembered the many stories of God's deliverance.
His prayer recalled moments of profound mercy. The prophet's
prayer was praise-filled and saw Habakkuk looking at the desolation
of his country while holding on to future hope with a strong grip.

The prophet recognized God as merciful, and in the midst
of justice, exile might well have been the most merciful choice.
Devastation weakened to disappointment, which led to the
discovery of a hope that welcomed mercy.

Restoration had already begun.

Revive us, O Lord, that Your people may rejoice in You!

The Lord's Prayer

Our Father which art in heaven, hallowed be thy name.
MATTHEW 6:9

Read through enough prayers and you may not find a discernible pattern or formula. Maybe this is because prayer is conversation with God and not all conversations follow a set pattern. Sometimes you have no idea what to say. Sometimes your prayers feature two desperate words: "Help me!"

This prayer from the Son of God featured some of the most desirable elements of prayer.

> "Our Father which art in heaven, hallowed be thy name. Thy kingdom come, Thy will be done in earth, as it is in heaven" (Matthew 6:9–10). *God comes first.*
>
> "Give us this day our daily bread" (verse 11). *God provides.*
>
> "And forgive us our debts, as we forgive our debtors" (verse 12). *God forgives. So must we.*
>
> "And lead us not into temptation, but deliver us from evil" (verse 13). *God's protection from evil should be regularly requested and never assumed.*

The Lord's Prayer is more than just a prayer to recite in honor of the Author. It is a reminder that when the prayer says "us," we should think of others. When we say, "Your kingdom come," we remember that we seek God's kingdom not ours. When we ask God to give us "daily bread," we acknowledge that He is able to meet our needs.

Between the familiar words of this prayer, we are reminded that our God conversations should focus on Him and the people He loves.

Holy Father, You have adopted us into Your family to be Your sons and daughters. May we love one another as You have loved us, and bear one another's burdens as members of one family.

A Soldier's Faith Prayer

Lord, I am not worthy that thou shouldest come under my roof:
but speak the word only, and my servant shall be healed.
MATTHEW 8:8

Behold a prayer from a most unusual source. The words were said in the accent of Rome. The speaker was an officer in the ruling army. The Jewish people were looking for a Messiah to remove just such a man from their midst.

This soldier could have been demanding, arrogant, and abusive. Instead, he expressed profound honor to Jesus who was, by law, supposed to obey him.

This was an extraordinary man. He genuinely cared for the servant in his home. He believed the stories that Jesus healed the sick. He had faith that if Jesus was willing, He could heal the young servant.

The faith of this Roman soldier was so strong, he suggested that if Jesus said the servant was healed, then that would be enough. He didn't want to disturb Jesus by making Him come to his home.

It is possible some Jewish people hoped Jesus would refuse this Gentile soldier, but Jesus said, "Go thy way; and as thou hast believed, so be it done unto thee. And his servant was healed in the selfsame hour" (Matthew 8:13).

God knew many would wonder if He were selective in His rescue plan. Would salvation only come to one people group? This answered prayer gives us another reason to believe the words, "For God so loved the world" (John 3:16).

Thank You, Father, that You don't show favoritism but accept
from all nations those who fear You and do what is right.
Your message of good news through peace with Jesus
Christ, who is Lord of all, is for all people.

A Leper Bowed Unclean

*And, behold, there came a leper and worshipped him,
saying, Lord, if thou wilt, thou canst make me clean.*
MATTHEW 8:2

Old Testament law had provisions for dealing with those who had wasting skin diseases, generally called leprosy. People were afraid to come in contact with them, because to associate with a leper might mean they would contract the disease. To contract the disease could mean living the rest of their lives as outcasts and having to call out "Unclean" whenever healthy people came near.

It is not hard to imagine people rushing to avoid a leper. They routinely lived in colonies outside the city and away from those with clear complexions.

In this prayer an *unclean* man responded in faith—not fear. He should have called out his traditional warning, but he resorted to a broken beggar's prayer. What was Jesus' response? "Jesus put forth his hand, and touched him, saying, I will; be thou clean. And immediately his leprosy was cleansed" (Matthew 8:3).

We don't know how long this man lived with the disease, but because he was *covered* with leprosy, the disease likely stood between himself and his family. It certainly stood between himself and a normal life.

His faith acknowledged that Jesus could heal him. The bold face-to-the-ground faith-filled prayer of an outcast is a reminder that sometimes we don't have something because we haven't asked (see James 4:3).

*May we never forget all the benefits You provide for us, Lord. You
forgive all of our sins and heal all of our diseases. You redeem our
lives from the pit and crown us with love and compassion.*

A Woman's Audacious Faith

For she said within herself,
If I may but touch his garment, I shall be whole.
MATTHEW 9:21

Jesus rescued a demon-possessed man and was on His way to raise a twelve-year-old girl from the dead. On the way, the crowd pressed in and Jesus stopped to ask a peculiar question: "Who touched my clothes?" (Mark 5:30).

Maybe Jesus wanted the culprit to admit what he or she had done, but He was God's Son and He knew who touched His robe—and why. The disciples said there was no way of knowing. Perhaps they had forgotten who He was.

The woman stood trembling, knowing her prayer had been answered. She was healed. She had spent twelve years with a debilitating disease that left her unclean. Medical treatments had left her funds totally depleted. She tried everything she could think of for healing and ultimately came to what she may have felt was a choice of last resort. Her words, however, indicate an audacity of faith that Jesus recognized when she touched His robe.

Jesus' words must have been filled with compassionate mercy. "Daughter, be of good comfort; thy faith hath made thee whole" (Matthew 9:22).

Each of us deals with painful physical wounds and deep emotional scars. We may think we have nowhere left to turn, but we all long to understand the truth of Jesus' words, "Thy faith hath made thee whole."

Father, forgive us when we run to the medicine cabinet or
the doctor's office before we come to You to ask for healing.
Your Word teaches us that by Jesus' wounds we are healed.
May we learn to trust in You and submit to
whatever healing process You choose to use.

Jesus Heals Two Blind Men

Then touched he their eyes, saying,
According to your faith be it unto you.
MATTHEW 9:29

Crowds often followed Jesus as He journeyed from place to place. His fame had spread throughout the land as He taught the people and worked miracles among them. He had recently healed a woman with bleeding issues and raised a young girl from the dead. One day two blind men followed Him, crying out for His attention. "Thou Son of David, have mercy on us" (Matthew 9:27). They followed Jesus into a house. Once inside, Jesus turned to them and asked, "Do you believe that I am able to do this?"

"Yes, Lord," they answered.

Jesus honored their faith by praying for them. "Then touched he their eyes, saying, According to your faith be it unto you" (Matthew 9:29). Sight was restored to the two blind men because they believed Jesus could do what they asked.

After He healed them, Jesus warned the two men, "See that no man know it" (verse 30). They paid no attention to what He said. They had just received a miracle. They could see, maybe for the first time in their lives. They went out and spread the word in the whole region, telling the story of how Jesus had given them sight.

Lord, increase our faith to believe that all things are
possible with You, and give us boldness to proclaim it.

Jesus Gives Thanks to God

I thank thee, O Father, Lord of heaven and earth.
MATTHEW 11:25

Jesus spent time in prayer with His Father during His thirty-three years on earth. In this verse, He is seen offering a prayer of thanksgiving to His Father. As Jesus was teaching the multitudes in the towns of Galilee, He told them of the judgment they could expect because they didn't repent. Then He thanked God for revealing His teachings unto children instead of the educated people of that day. "I thank thee, O Father, Lord of heaven and earth, because thou hast hid these things from the wise and prudent, and hast revealed them unto babes" (Matthew 11:25).

Children came to Him in innocence, desiring to learn. Those who are wise and educated often have their minds made up in advance and are not willing to change. Jesus had been teaching them about their need for repentance, but they had not turned from their sin in spite of His miracles.

The prayer Jesus offered to His Father ended with the statement, "Even so, Father: for so it seemed good in thy sight" (verse 26). Jesus always sought the perfect will of God. He knew His Father's will had been to reveal His purpose to children.

*Lord, help us come to You as children, realizing our need
to repent; seeking Your will and not our own.*

Peter's Prayer to Walk on Water

And Peter answered him and said, Lord,
if it be thou, bid me come unto thee on the water.
MATTHEW 14:28

After Jesus performed the miracle of feeding the five thousand with the five loaves and two fish, He told His disciples to get into a ship and go to the other side of the lake. Then Jesus sent the multitude away and went up into a mountain to pray. He was there alone until evening.

Meanwhile, the disciples, who had sailed a considerable distance, encountered a storm on the sea. High waves and wind threatened to shipwreck them. Some of these men were fishermen who knew the power of a storm. Into the middle of this fearful chaos came Jesus walking on the water. The disciples thought He was a ghost. Now they not only faced shipwreck but an unknown image on the water. They cried out in their fear, but Jesus spoke, reassuring them that it was He. "Be of good cheer; it is I; be not afraid" (Matthew 14:27).

Peter decided to put courage to the test. He said, "Lord, if it be thou, bid me come unto thee on the water" (verse 28). Jesus answered this prayer with one word: "Come" (verse 29). In response to this word from His Master, Peter stepped out of the boat and into the water.

Lord, at Your word, may we take courage to get out
of the boat and step into the water.

Peter Prays for Help

But when he saw the wind boisterous, he was afraid;
and beginning to sink, he cried, saying, Lord, save me.
Matthew 14:30

In the middle of a ferocious storm, Jesus walked on the water toward His disciples in their boat. When Peter heard the voice of Jesus telling him to come to Him on the water, he stepped out of the boat. At first he walked on the water toward Jesus, but then he looked at his surroundings. He saw the wind whipping the water, and it scared him. When he took his eyes off Jesus and looked at the storm, he began to sink into the sea. Peter was a fisherman, so he probably knew how to swim, but fear had taken over. Peter's prayer for help was simple. He didn't have time to speak great flowing words; he simply cried out, "Lord, save me" (Matthew 14:30). Jesus immediately reached out to Peter and rescued him from the treacherous water beneath them.

Jesus rebuked Peter for his fear, asking him why he doubted. Matthew doesn't tell us what Peter answered or if he responded to the question. But one thing is certain: Peter knew who to call on in time of need. Sometimes people get into trouble by looking at their circumstances and allowing fear to overtake them.

Lord, help us realize there is no storm too great for You
to rescue us. We can call on You in any circumstance.

A Canaanite Woman Asks for Help

And, behold, a woman of Canaan came out of the same coasts,
and cried unto him, saying, Have mercy on me, O Lord,
thou son of David; my daughter is grievously vexed with a devil.
MATTHEW 15:22

As Jesus traveled in the region of Tyre and Sidon, a Canaanite woman approached him, crying out for help. She recognized who He was and called Him "Lord, thou son of David." Her request for help was for her demon-possessed daughter. Jesus ignored her pleas at first, but her incessant cries annoyed His disciples. They asked Jesus to send her away. Jesus answered them by saying that He had been sent only to the lost sheep of Israel.

The woman refused to give up. She was desperate to find help for her daughter. She came to Jesus again, knelt, and worshipped Him, saying, "Lord, help me" (Matthew 15:25). His answer might have sent a less-determined person away. He replied, "It is not meet to take the children's bread, and to cast it to dogs" (verse 26). Still she persisted. "Truth, Lord: yet the dogs eat of the crumbs which fall from their masters' table" (verse 27). When Jesus heard this reply, He told her she had great faith and rewarded her faith by healing her daughter that very moment.

Sometimes we don't get an answer as quickly as we want, but like the Canaanite woman, we must not give up. God honors our faith in Him.

Lord, increase our faith in Your ability
to heal and deliver those who call on You.

A Mother's Request for Her Sons

She saith unto him, Grant that these my two sons may sit,
the one on thy right hand, and the other on
the left, in thy kingdom.
MATTHEW 20:21

The wife of Zebedee, along with her sons, James and John, approached Jesus with a request: that one would sit on Jesus' right and the other on His left. Jesus responded that they didn't know what they were asking. Could they partake of the things required of Him? "Are ye able to drink of the cup that I shall drink of?" (Matthew 20:22).

"We are able," they answered. He said, yes, they would be partakers, but assigning the seats on His right hand and left hand wasn't His responsibility. His Father would make those decisions (see verse 23).

The other ten disciples were indignant at the selfish request made by James and John, but Jesus had some advice for all of them. They were to be different. They weren't to be like the Gentiles of that day. He didn't want them to be rulers over each other; He wanted them to minister in the same way He ministered to people. If they desired to be great, they had to serve. "Whosoever will be chief among you, let him be your servant" (verse 27).

James and John had ambitions, but Jesus wanted them to keep their priorities in order.

Lord, teach us to order our priorities according
to Your will, and give us a heart to serve.

Crowds Praise Jesus

*Hosanna to the son of David: Blessed is he that cometh
in the name of the Lord; Hosanna in the highest.*
MATTHEW 21:9

Jesus and His disciples were traveling to Jerusalem where He would be tried and crucified. Before they went into Jerusalem, He sent two of the disciples to a nearby village to get a donkey and her colt. "If any man say ought unto you, ye shall say, The Lord hath need of them; and straightway he will send them" (Matthew 21:3). When they returned, they placed their cloaks on the donkey so Jesus could sit on the animal. A large crowd of His followers had gathered, and they spread their cloaks on the road Jesus was to travel. Others cut tree branches and laid them on the path.

As the crowd moved toward Jerusalem, they began to shout praises to Jesus. "Hosanna to the son of David: Blessed is he that cometh in the name of the Lord; Hosanna in the highest" (verse 9). Without reservation, they praised the Lord with their actions and their words. As Jesus entered Jerusalem, the entire city was stirred by the praise and worship of this man. People began asking, "Who is this?" (verse 10).

"Jesus the prophet of Nazareth of Galilee," the crowd responded (verse 11).

The crowd that accompanied Jesus on His entry into Jerusalem made it known who Jesus was, and they worshipped Him openly.

*Lord, give us the courage and boldness to proclaim
You as Lord and Savior to the world around us.*

Jesus Prays When Crucified

*And about the ninth hour Jesus cried with a loud voice,
saying, Eli, Eli, lama sabachthani? that is to say, My God,
my God, why hast thou forsaken me?*
MATTHEW 27:46

Jesus knew His purpose on earth from the beginning—that He would be offered as a sacrifice for many. A sacrifice that He made willingly. As He hung on the cross enduring untold agony for the sins of the world, darkness fell over the land. This darkness lasted for three hours—from noon until three in the afternoon. About three o'clock, Jesus prayed to the Father, "Eli, Eli, lama sabachthani? that is to say, My God, my God, why hast thou forsaken me?" (Matthew 27:46).

Jesus had taken on the sins of the whole world, and a holy God could not look on that sin. Even though He called out in the midst of great suffering, Jesus knew He was fulfilling the will of His Father. Even as He prayed those words, He knew God was present. "Jesus, when he had cried again with a loud voice, yielded up the ghost" (verse 50). His purpose on earth had been fulfilled, His work finished. Soon He would rejoin the Father in heaven, having completed His mission.

At times we may feel God has forsaken us. The trials are long and hard. Even though we can't see Him working, He is present.

*Lord, help us by faith to accept Your presence
and faithfulness in our lives.*

Jesus Rebukes an Unclean Spirit

*And there was in their synagogue a man with an unclean spirit;
and he cried out, saying, Let us alone; what have we to do with
thee, thou Jesus of Nazareth? art thou come to destroy us?
I know thee who thou art, the Holy One of God. And Jesus
rebuked him, saying, Hold thy peace, and come out of him.*
MARK 1:23–25

In their travels, Jesus and His disciples journeyed to Capernaum.
On the Sabbath day, Jesus entered the synagogue and taught the
people. His teaching amazed those in attendance that day. He
didn't sound like any of the teachers of the law they usually listened
to; this man spoke with great authority.

One of the people in attendance that day was a man with an
unclean spirit. As he listened to Jesus teaching, he cried out, "What
have we to do with thee, thou Jesus of Nazareth? art thou come to
destroy us? I know thee who thou art, the Holy One of God" (Mark
1:24). Jesus immediately took control. "Jesus rebuked him, saying,
Hold thy peace, and come out of him" (verse 25). The unclean spirit
was subject to Jesus. He came out of the man with a shriek. The
people were amazed not only at His teaching but at His authority
over unclean spirits. News about this miraculous deliverance spread
throughout the region.

The man with the unclean spirit was changed when he met
Jesus. Whatever enemies we may face, they are subject to the power
and authority of Jesus also.

*Lord, help us to let go of the strongholds
in our lives and give You control.*

The Disciples Pray for Safety

*And there arose a great storm of wind, and the waves beat into
the ship, so that it was now full. And he was in the hinder
part of the ship, asleep on a pillow: and they awake him,
and say unto him, Master, carest thou not that we perish?*
MARK 4:37–38

After a day of teaching, Jesus said to His disciples, "Let us pass
over unto the other side" (Mark 4:35). They boarded a ship and
left the crowd behind, sailing out into the sea. Some smaller boats
accompanied them. Jesus, evidently tired from the day, went to
another part of the ship and lay down.

While Jesus slept, a furious storm arose. The wind blew with
great force, and the waves broke over the side of the ship, filling it
with water. Afraid for their lives, the disciples awoke Jesus. Their
prayer came in the form of a question: "Master, carest thou not that
we perish?" (verse 38).

Jesus arose and rebuked the storm: "Peace, be still" (verse 39).
Then Jesus had a question for them. "Why are ye so fearful? how
is it that ye have no faith?" (verse 40). Jesus wanted them to believe
in Him.

The disciples had been afraid of the storm, but now they were
terrified. Who was this man that even the wind and the waves
obeyed Him? The man they spent time with every day was more
than just a teacher. He had power and authority over the elements.

*Lord, increase our faith, and help us realize that You are
all we need in every storm that blows against our ship.*

Jesus Prays for a Demon-Possessed Man

And cried with a loud voice, and said, What have I to do with thee, Jesus, thou Son of the most high God? I adjure thee by God, that thou torment me not. For he said unto him, Come out of the man, thou unclean spirit.

MARK 5:7–8

Jesus sailed by ship into the country of the Gadarenes. When He arrived, a demon-possessed man who lived in a nearby cemetery came out to meet Him. His possession was so great, he could not be subdued. The people in the area had already tried to chain him, but he broke the chains and freed himself.

As soon as he saw Jesus, he ran, fell to his knees and worshipped Him. Jesus commanded the unclean spirit to come out of the man (see Mark 5:6, 8).

The demon spirit spoke. He shouted at the top of his voice, "What have I to do with thee, Jesus, thou Son of the most high God? I adjure thee by God, that thou torment me not" (verse 7).

"What is thy name?" Jesus asked (verse 9).

"My name is Legion: for we are many," he replied (verse 9).

The unclean spirit recognized Jesus as the Son of God and knew he was subject unto Him. The devils in Legion begged Jesus to send them into some pigs feeding nearby. "Forthwith Jesus gave them leave. And the unclean spirits went out, and entered into the swine: and the herd ran violently down a steep place into the sea, (they were about two thousand;) and were choked in the sea" (verse 13).

Lord, may we recognize Your power over all things in our lives so that we can have victory through You.

Jairus Prays for His Daughter's Healing

*And, behold, there cometh one of the rulers of the synagogue,
Jairus by name; and when he saw him, he fell at his feet,
and besought him greatly, saying, My little daughter lieth
at the point of death: I pray thee, come and lay thy hands
on her, that she may be healed; and she shall live.*

Mark 5:22–23

A leader of the synagogue named Jairus had a twelve-year-old
daughter who was dying. He approached Jesus one day and begged
Him for help. "My little daughter lieth at the point of death: I pray
thee, come and lay thy hands on her, that she may be healed" (Mark
5:23).

Jesus agreed to go with him. On the way, Jesus was delayed
by the crowds and others wanting to touch Him. While Jesus was
talking with others, someone came and told Jairus that his daughter
had died and not to bother Jesus anymore. "As soon as Jesus heard
the word that was spoken, he saith unto the ruler of the synagogue,
Be not afraid, only believe" (verse 36).

Jesus made His way to Jairus's house and went inside. A crowd
had gathered, crying and wailing in grief. Jesus asked them why
they were crying so. When He told them she wasn't dead, only
sleeping, they laughed at Him. He went into the room where
the girl was and took her by the hand and said, "Talitha cumi;
which is, being interpreted, Damsel, I say unto thee, arise" (verse
41). She stood and began to walk around. Jesus commanded that
"something should be given her to eat" (verse 43). She was healed
and resurrected by God's power.

*Lord, You have power even over death. Because You live,
we can live also. Thank You for eternal life.*

Jesus Heals a Deaf Mute

And they bring unto him one that was deaf, and had an impediment in his speech; and they beseech him to put his hand upon him. And he took him aside from the multitude, and put his fingers into his ears, and he spit, and touched his tongue; and looking up to heaven, he sighed, and saith unto him, Ephphatha, that is, Be opened.

MARK 7:32–34

A deaf man who also had a speech impediment was brought to Jesus. The people bringing him wanted Jesus to put His hands on the man. The crowd knew that all it took for healing was just a touch of Jesus' hands.

Jesus took the man away from the multitude and put his fingers into his ears, then spit and touched his tongue. He prayed a short, one-word prayer for the man and his ears opened and he was able to speak. "Looking up to heaven, he sighed, and saith unto him, Ephphatha, that is, Be opened" (Mark 7:34).

Jesus' actions and short prayer may seem a bit unorthodox to some. Maybe that was why he moved the man away from the crowd. We are not given the reason for these methods; the deaf mute didn't seem to object though. He allowed Jesus to do His work. The important thing is that the man was healed. Jesus told the people not to tell what had happened, but the more He told them not to, the more they talked about it. They were amazed at His miracles.

Lord, help us resist questioning Your answers or Your ways in our lives, and trust that You will always do what is necessary, knowing that You will do it well.

Bartimaeus Prays for Sight

And when he heard that it was Jesus of Nazareth, he began to cry out, and say, Jesus, thou son of David, have mercy on me. And many charged him that he should hold his peace: but he cried the more a great deal, Thou son of David, have mercy on me.
MARK 10:47–48

As Jesus and His followers left the city of Jericho one day, a blind man named Bartimaeus sat by the side of the road begging. People passed him every day. He couldn't see them, but he could hear them talking. On this particular day, he heard that Jesus of Nazareth, the healer, was in the crowd.

Bartimaeus saw his chance and shouted, "Jesus, thou son of David, have mercy on me" (Mark 10:47).

The crowd told him to be quiet. They felt Jesus didn't have time for a beggar.

That didn't stop Bartimaeus. He shouted even more: "Son of David, have mercy on me" (verse 48).

Jesus stopped and commanded that Bartimaeus be called. Bartimaeus threw his cloak to one side, jumped to his feet, and came to Jesus.

"Jesus answered and said unto him, What wilt thou that I should do unto thee? The blind man said unto him, Lord, that I might receive my sight" (verse 51).

"Go thy way; thy faith hath made thee whole," Jesus said (verse 52). Immediately, Bartimaeus could see and began following Jesus. If Bartimaeus had listened to the crowd that day, he would have missed his miracle.

It is easy to listen to the crowd sometimes and make the wrong move.

Lord, help us never be afraid to call on You, no matter what others think, and always be ready to receive Your answer.

Simeon Sees Jesus

*Lord, now lettest thou thy servant depart in peace, according
to thy word: For mine eyes have seen thy salvation, which thou
hast prepared before the face of all people; a light to lighten
the Gentiles, and the glory of thy people Israel.*
LUKE 2:29–32

An elderly man named Simeon had been told by the Holy Spirit
that he would not die before he had seen the Messiah (Luke 2:26).
He was a devout man who followed the direction of the Holy
Spirit in his life. He believed this promise.

Shortly after Jesus' birth, when it came time for Jesus to be
circumcised, Joseph and Mary brought Him to the temple in
Jerusalem to present Him to the Lord and to offer a sacrifice
according to the law. Simeon, directed by the Holy Spirit to go to
the temple, was there when Joseph and Mary came in with Jesus.

Simeon took the Christ Child into His arms and said, "Lord,
now lettest thou thy servant depart in peace, according to thy word"
(verse 29). Simeon knew by the Holy Spirit that he was holding
the promised Messiah in his arms. "For mine eyes have seen thy
salvation, which thou hast prepared before the face of all people;
a light to lighten the Gentiles, and the glory of thy people Israel"
(verses 30–32). Simeon was now ready to die. He had seen the
Messiah. He had received His promise.

*Lord, may we, like Simeon, be directed by the Holy Spirit in our
lives and believe the promises given to us through Your Word.*

Jesus Heals a Demon-Possessed Boy

And, behold, a man of the company cried out, saying, Master,
I beseech thee, look upon my son: for he is mine only child.
And, lo, a spirit taketh him, and he suddenly crieth out;
and it teareth him that he foameth again, and bruising him
hardly departeth from him. And I besought thy disciples
to cast him out; and they could not.
LUKE 9:38–40

The day after His transfiguration, Jesus and the men with Him came down from the mountain. A large crowd met them at the bottom. One of those people was a man who had a demon-possessed boy. He called out to Jesus and described the problem to Him. "A spirit taketh him, and he suddenly crieth out; and it teareth him that he foameth again, and bruising him hardly departeth from him" (Luke 9:39).

The man went on to say that he had asked Jesus' disciples to cast out the demon, but they couldn't do it. "I besought thy disciples to cast him out; and they could not" (verse 40).

"Bring thy son hither," Jesus told him (verse 41).

While the boy was coming to Jesus, the demon threw him on the ground in a convulsion. "Jesus rebuked the unclean spirit, healed the child, and delivered him again to his father" (verse 42). The people in the crowd were amazed at the power of God manifested through Jesus as He healed the boy. Would people in the twenty-first century be as amazed at the power of Jesus if He walked among us today?

Lord, help us realize You have the same power
today as when You lived on earth.

Jesus Teaches His Disciples to Pray

And he said unto them, When ye pray, say, Our Father which
art in heaven, hallowed be thy name. Thy kingdom come.
Thy will be done, as in heaven, so in earth. Give us day by
day our daily bread. And forgive us our sins; for we also
forgive every one that is indebted to us. And lead us
not into temptation; but deliver us from evil.

LUKE 11:2–4

The disciples asked Jesus to teach them to pray, as John had taught his disciples. Jesus' response was to give them a prayer and teach them about God's provision. "He said unto them, When ye pray, say, Our Father which art in heaven, hallowed be thy name" (Luke 11:2). They were to acknowledge the Father then continue by asking for their daily bread and forgiveness of sins.

Jesus asked His disciples what they would do if a friend showed up at midnight asking for something to eat for unexpected company. Even though the friend and his family were already in bed, because the knocker persisted in his request, the friend would get out of bed and give him what he needed.

Jesus said if they asked, they would receive. "I say unto you, Ask, and it shall be given you; seek, and ye shall find; knock, and it shall be opened unto you" (verse 9). Jesus went on to say that if they knew how to give to their children, then how much more would God give to those who ask Him?

Lord, help us trust in You, knowing You will
provide for us just as we provide for our families.

The Rich Man Asks for Relief

*And in hell he lift up his eyes, being in torments, and seeth Abraham
afar off, and Lazarus in his bosom. And he cried and said,
Father Abraham, have mercy on me, and send Lazarus,
that he may dip the tip of his finger in water, and cool my
tongue; for I am tormented in this flame.*
LUKE 16:23–24

A rich man had every luxury he could want while a beggar named
Lazarus laid outside his gate hoping to eat the leftover crumbs
from the rich man's table. One day Lazarus died and was carried by
angels into Abraham's bosom. The rich man died also, but he went
to hell. He could see Lazarus at rest in Abraham's bosom while the
rich man was being tormented. He cried out for help.

"Father Abraham, have mercy on me, and send Lazarus, that
he may dip the tip of his finger in water, and cool my tongue; for I
am tormented in this flame" (Luke 16:24).

Abraham's reply came back: "Son, remember that thou in thy
lifetime receivedst thy good things, and likewise Lazarus evil things:
but now he is comforted, and thou art tormented" (verse 25).

The rich man then requested that he send Lazarus to his
five brothers to warn them so they wouldn't join him in hell.
But Abraham said they had Moses and the prophets, and if they
wouldn't hear them, they wouldn't hear someone who returned
from the dead.

The rich man had every opportunity on earth to do the right
thing, but he allowed that opportunity to pass, and now all was lost.

*Father, help us seize the opportunity to live
for You while here on earth.*

Ten Lepers Pray for Healing

And as he entered into a certain village, there met him ten
men that were lepers, which stood afar off: and they lifted
up their voices, and said, Jesus, Master, have mercy on us.
LUKE 17:12–13

As Jesus entered a village located on the border between Galilee and Samaria, ten lepers met Him. People who had leprosy were considered unclean and had to keep a certain distance between themselves and others, so they stood at a distance from Jesus and called out to Him in a loud voice: "Jesus, Master, have mercy on us" (Luke 17:13). His response to them: "Go shew yourselves unto the priests" (verse 14).

Under the law of Moses, the priest had to declare someone clean. Jesus' response to the lepers was the answer to their prayer. They had to go to the priest and let him declare them clean from their leprosy—confirmation that Jesus had healed them. As they obeyed Jesus and went to the priest, they were cleansed from their disease.

One of the lepers who saw that he had been healed came back to Jesus praising God. He threw himself at Jesus' feet and thanked Him. "Jesus answering said, Were there not ten cleansed? but where are the nine? There are not found that returned to give glory to God, save this stranger" (verses 17–18). Jesus said to this man, "Arise, go thy way: thy faith hath made thee whole" (verse 19).

Lord, may we always remember to praise You
and give thanks for what You do for us.

The Pharisee Exalts Himself in Prayer

*The Pharisee stood and prayed thus with himself, God,
I thank thee, that I am not as other men are, extortioners,
unjust, adulterers, or even as this publican. I fast twice
in the week, I give tithes of all that I possess.*
LUKE 18:11–12

As Jesus taught, He came in contact with some who thought they were righteous and looked down on everyone else. Pharisees set themselves apart, thinking they were better than others. They were very strict in keeping every point of the Law of Moses, yet their religion was more of a formality than a sincere dedication to God. They were opposed to Jesus and His teachings and were some of His fiercest enemies. Jesus often rebuked them along with the Sadducees for their hypocrisy. He told a story of a Pharisee who went into the temple to pray: "The Pharisee stood and prayed thus with himself, God, I thank thee, that I am not as other men are, extortioners, unjust, adulterers, or even as this publican" (Luke 18:11). He went on to brag about his fasting and how much he gave in tithes.

Jesus said that those who exalt themselves will be humbled. The Pharisee went home unjustified in God's eyes. He had deceived himself into thinking he was above others.

*Lord, help us realize we are nothing without You.
Help us submit ourselves to You rather than
boasting of our own accomplishments.*

The Tax Collector's Prayer

*And the publican, standing afar off, would not lift up so
much as his eyes unto heaven, but smote upon his breast,
saying, God be merciful to me a sinner.*
LUKE 18:13

Publicans, or tax collectors, as they were known, were considered
some of the lowest people in biblical times. They were hired by
the Romans to collect taxes on goods exported and imported into
Israel. They overcharged and cheated people to make an extra profit
for themselves. They falsely accused people of smuggling in order
to get hush money. Many thought of the tax collectors as traitors to
their own countrymen.

When the tax collector in Jesus' story entered the temple, he
had a different attitude than the Pharisee who thought he was
above sin and superior to others. The tax collector stood off to one
side at a distance and wouldn't even lift his eyes toward heaven. He
knew what he was as he stood before God, and he acknowledged it.
Instead, he "smote upon his breast, saying, God be merciful to me
a sinner" (Luke 18:13).

Jesus responded to this prayer by saying that this sinner
returned home justified before God. He had approached God in
humility rather than pride: "For every one that exalteth himself
shall be abased; and he that humbleth himself shall be exalted"
(verse 14).

*Lord, may we humble ourselves before You, realizing our need
for Your mercy. Help us exalt You in our lives.*

Jesus Prays at the Mount of Olives

And he came out, and went, as he was wont, to the mount of Olives;
and his disciples also followed him. And when he was at the place,
he said unto them, Pray that ye enter not into temptation. And he
was withdrawn from them about a stone's cast, and kneeled down,
and prayed, saying, Father, if thou be willing, remove this cup
from me: nevertheless not my will, but thine, be done.
LUKE 22:39–42

After the Passover with His disciples, Jesus left the Upper Room and went to the Mount of Olives to pray. His disciples followed Him, and He instructed them to pray also that they wouldn't fall into temptation. Jesus knew what lay ahead not only for Himself but for those who followed Him.

Jesus left His disciples and walked about a stone's throw away from them to pray. He was facing death, but He prayed for His Father's will: "Father, if thou be willing, remove this cup from me: nevertheless not my will, but thine, be done" (Luke 22:42). In response to His prayer, an angel from heaven appeared to Him and strengthened Him (verse 43).

Jesus continued to pray in such agony that His sweat fell to the ground as though it were drops of blood. When at last Jesus stood and went back to where He had left the disciples, they were all asleep. He woke them and once again instructed them to pray. They didn't realize just how much they needed the strength for the time ahead.

Lord, help us avoid being negligent in our prayer lives,
because prayer is our source of strength in times of temptation.

Jesus Prays for His Enemies

*And when they were come to the place, which is called Calvary,
there they crucified him, and the malefactors, one on the right
hand, and the other on the left. Then said Jesus, Father,
forgive them; for they know not what they do.*

Luke 23:33–34

After a cruel mock trial and appearances before the leaders in Jerusalem, Jesus was given His cross to carry in procession toward Calvary. On the way there, Simon, a man from Cyrene, happened to be coming into town from the country, and the soldiers stopped him. They laid the cross on his shoulders, and he followed Jesus to Calvary.

When they reached the place called the Skull, the soldiers crucified Jesus along with two criminals, one on either side of Him. As He hung on the cross, Jesus prayed for the ones carrying out His sentence: "Father, forgive them; for they know not what they do" (Luke 23:34). The soldiers He prayed for gambled for His clothing as He prayed, not realizing who they had nailed to the cross above them. He loved them even in their mockery of Him.

The prayer Jesus prayed on the cross offered forgiveness to His enemies, and His sacrifice brought salvation to the world. "For if, when we were enemies, we were reconciled to God by the death of his Son, much more, being reconciled, we shall be saved by his life" (Romans 5:10). Jesus gave the ultimate gift so all mankind might have life.

*Thank You, Jesus, for the gift of salvation made
possible by Your death on the cross.*

Jesus Commends His Spirit to God

And when Jesus had cried with a loud voice, he said,
Father, into thy hands I commend my spirit:
and having said thus, he gave up the ghost.
LUKE 23:46

When Jesus was crucified, darkness covered the earth for about three hours, from noon until three o'clock. During this time, the veil of the temple, which covered the entrance to the Holy of Holies, was torn in two. The way had been made for man to enter this holy place and have communion with God one on one. When this happened, Jesus prayed with a loud voice to the Father.

"When Jesus had cried with a loud voice, he said, Father, into thy hands I commend my spirit: and having said thus, he gave up the ghost" (Luke 23:46). The Roman centurion in charge of the execution witnessed this event and realized they had crucified an innocent man (see verse 47). But the death of Jesus was not in vain. He came to this earth with the purpose of giving His life for all mankind. He commended His Spirit into His Father's hands, knowing that all was well and the work had been completed.

Father, help us place our lives and all that we have into
Your hands, knowing You will see us through to the end.

The Woman at the Well
Asks for Living Water

The woman saith unto him, Sir, give me this water,
that I thirst not, neither come hither to draw.
JOHN 4:15

While traveling through Samaria, Jesus and His disciples stopped in a city called Sychar where Jacob's well was located. Jesus waited at the well while His disciples went to buy food. When a Samaritan woman came to draw water, Jesus asked for a drink. Jews didn't associate with Samaritans, so the woman questioned Him as to why He was asking her for a drink.

Jesus said if she knew who was asking her for water, she could ask Him and He would give her living water (see John 4:10). If she drank of the water He offered, she would never thirst again (verse 14).

The woman said, "Sir, give me this water, that I thirst not, neither come hither to draw" (verse 15).

As they talked, the woman recognized Jesus was much more than a man wanting a drink of water. She recognized Him as a prophet and the promised Messiah.

"The woman saith unto him, I know that Messias cometh, which is called Christ: when he is come, he will tell us all things. Jesus saith unto her, I that speak unto thee am he" (verses 25–26).

Lord, help us drink of the living water You so freely
offer and then lead others to the well.

A Royal Official Asks for His Son's Healing

The nobleman saith unto him, Sir,
come down ere my child die.
JOHN 4:49

The people of Galilee welcomed Jesus into their region. They had been in Jerusalem during the Passover celebration and knew about Him and His ministry. Jesus went to the city of Cana in Galilee where He had turned the water into wine.

A government official approached Jesus about his son. "When he heard that Jesus was come out of Judaea into Galilee, he went unto him, and besought him that he would come down, and heal his son: for he was at the point of death" (John 4:47).

Jesus told the man that unless the people see signs and wonders, they would never believe. The man continued to plead with Jesus. "Sir, come down ere my child die" (John 4:49).

Jesus told him to go, that his son would live. The man took Jesus at His word and started home. On his way home, one of his servants met him and reported that his son was alive.

"Then enquired he of them the hour when he began to amend. And they said unto him, Yesterday at the seventh hour the fever left him" (verse 52). The man realized that it was the exact time Jesus had told him his son would live.

Lord, give us faith to take You at Your word
and accept what You have promised us.

Jesus Gives Thanks to God for Hearing

Then they took away the stone from the place where the dead was laid.
And Jesus lifted up his eyes, and said, Father, I thank thee that thou
hast heard me. And I knew that thou hearest me always:
but because of the people which stand by I said it,
that they may believe that thou hast sent me.

JOHN 11:41–42

When Lazarus, a friend of Jesus, became sick, Mary and Martha sent word to Jesus. He did not immediately go to Bethany but waited two days. When Jesus arrived, He learned Lazarus had died. Martha met Him and said, "Lord, if thou hadst been here, my brother had not died" (John 11:21). Jesus responded to her by saying that her brother would rise again.

Jesus asked where Lazarus was buried, and they took Him to the tomb, which had a stone covering the opening. Jesus told them to roll the stone to one side (see verse 39). So they took away the stone, and Jesus prayed. "Father, I thank thee that thou hast heard me. And I knew that thou hearest me always: but because of the people which stand by I said it, that they may believe that thou hast sent me" (verses 41–42). After He prayed, Jesus called out in a loud voice, "Lazarus, come forth" (verse 43). In response to the prayer and voice of Jesus, Lazarus came out of the tomb. "He that was dead came forth, bound hand and foot with graveclothes: and his face was bound about with a napkin. Jesus saith unto them, Loose him, and let him go" (verse 44).

Lord, let us hear and respond to Your
voice wherever we may be.

Jesus Prays That God's Name Be Glorified

*Now is my soul troubled; and what shall I say? Father,
save me from this hour: but for this cause came I unto this
hour. Father, glorify thy name. Then came there a voice from
heaven, saying, I have both glorified it, and will glorify it again.*
JOHN 12:27–28

Jesus had people following Him everywhere He went. Some had witnessed the resurrection of Lazarus, and others who had heard what He did met Jesus as He made His glorious entry into Jerusalem amid the cries of *hosanna*. Some Greeks who had come to Jerusalem for the feast told Philip they would like to see Jesus. When Philip and Andrew told Jesus, He answered them by saying, "The hour is come, that the Son of man should be glorified" (John 12:23). Jesus began to teach the disciples about being one of His followers and what it would mean, letting them know that to follow Him meant eternal life; but if they treasured their own life more than they loved Him, they would lose it.

After this Jesus prayed, "Father, glorify thy name" (verse 28). The Father responded from heaven, saying, "I have both glorified it, and will glorify it again" (verse 28). Some in the crowd thought it had thundered, but others said an angel had spoken to Jesus. The voice was for the benefit of the people around Him. Jesus knew the voice of the Father. He also knew what lay ahead of Him as He faced death on the cross.

*Lord, as Your people, help us recognize Your voice
and give You the honor and glory You deserve.*

Jesus Prays for Himself

And now, O Father, glorify thou me with thine own self
with the glory which I had with thee before the world was.
JOHN 17:5

As the time drew near for Jesus to face His purpose for coming
to earth, He told His disciples of the necessity that He go away
and what it would mean for them. It was for their own good that
He would be leaving, but He would send them an Advocate or
Comforter (see John 16:7). Jesus assured them that the sorrow they
felt would turn to joy again.

When Jesus finished speaking with the disciples, He lifted His
eyes toward heaven and began to pray: "Father, the hour is come;
glorify thy Son, that thy Son also may glorify thee" (John 17:1). Jesus
went on to pray about the authority given to Him to provide eternal
life for those who came to know God. He had brought glory to God
on earth by finishing the work He had been sent to do.

Jesus ended the prayer for Himself with one last statement:
"Glorify thou me with thine own self with the glory which I had
with thee before the world was" (verse 5). If Jesus felt the necessity
as the Son of God to pray for Himself, how much more should we
pray about our daily lives.

Lord, help us bring glory to You by doing
the work You have called us to do.

Jesus Prays for His Disciples

They are not of the world, even as I am not of the world.
Sanctify them through thy truth: thy word is truth. As thou hast
sent me into the world, even so have I also sent them into
the world. And for their sakes I sanctify myself, that they
also might be sanctified through the truth.
JOHN 17:16–19

Before Jesus went to Gethsemane, He spent time teaching His disciples and praying for them. He spoke to the Father about the men given to Him. Jesus had given them proof He was the Son of God. "For I have given unto them the words which thou gavest me; and they have received them, and have known surely that I came out from thee, and they have believed that thou didst send me" (John 17:8).

After this acknowledgment, Jesus began to pray for the disciples. "I pray for them: I pray not for the world, but for them which thou hast given me; for they are thine" (verse 9). Jesus wanted these men He loved to be protected as they went out into the world to preach the Gospel. While He was on earth, He had protected them, but now He would be leaving (see verse 12). "I pray not that thou shouldest take them out of the world, but that thou shouldest keep them from the evil. . . . Sanctify them through thy truth: thy word is truth" (verses 15, 17). The disciples could now go out to spread the Gospel under the protecting hand of God.

Lord, thank You for keeping us in Your care.

Jesus Desires Unity
among the Believers

*Thou, Father, art in me, and I in thee, that they also may be one
in us: that the world may believe that thou hast sent me.*
JOHN 17:21

Jesus spent much time in prayer for His disciples, but He didn't stop there. He commanded His disciples to spread the Gospel, and He knew this would bring others to Himself. So He prayed for unity among the brethren: "That they all may be one; as thou, Father, art in me, and I in thee, that they also may be one in us: that the world may believe that thou hast sent me" (John 17:21).

Over and over Jesus pleaded with the Father to bring unity. Why? So that others would believe, and glory would be brought to God. He had seen division even among His disciples (Matthew 20:20–28). He did not want this divisiveness because He knew it would be detrimental to His kingdom. Instead, He called for love and oneness: "I have declared unto them thy name, and will declare it: that the love wherewith thou hast loved me may be in them, and I in them" (John 17:26).

This world does not know the Father. It is opposite of all Christ desires, but those whom God has given to Jesus know that He is sent from the Father. This should bring us together as we strive to glorify Him.

*It is easy to notice petty differences, but, Lord,
let us love one another as You have loved us.*

The Disciples Seek God's Will

*And they prayed, and said, Thou, Lord, which knowest the hearts
of all men, shew whether of these two thou hast chosen.*
ACTS 1:24

Judas was gone. He had died with blood on his hands. Christ
had returned to heaven, and the apostles faced the daunting task
of choosing a replacement for Judas. Peter, the natural leader,
took charge of the situation. He reminded them that the events
surrounding Judas and the death of Jesus were all fulfillments of
prophecy and that Judas's place must be given to another: "Let his
days be few; and let another take his office" (Psalm 109:8).

How would they know who the right man would be? How
could they be sure they wouldn't choose another Judas? They
established some good criteria, but they knew it would be unwise
to proceed without God. When they had it narrowed down to two
men, they prayed: "Thou, Lord, which knowest the hearts of all
men, shew whether of these two thou hast chosen" (Acts 1:24).

In this instance, Judas's replacement was chosen by casting
lots. "They gave forth their lots; and the lot fell upon Matthias; and
he was numbered with the eleven apostles" (verse 26).

Often we are faced with decisions that seem impossible.
Maybe there are several good options, or perhaps there really don't
seem to be options. God knows what is right. He is just waiting
for us to ask.

*Some decisions are plain hard to make.
Father, help us always include You.*

The Apostles' Desire for Boldness

*And now, Lord, behold their threatenings: and grant unto thy
servants, that with all boldness they may speak thy word.*
ACTS 4:29

The Jews stood amazed. The man had been lame from birth, and here he was, over forty years old, running and leaping and praising God. Immediately Peter saw the opportunity. "Be it known unto you all, and to all the people of Israel, that by the name of Jesus Christ of Nazareth, whom ye crucified, whom God raised from the dead, even by him doth this man stand here before you whole" (Acts 4:10).

The religious leaders could see the truth in front of them, but it angered them, and all they could think to do was arrest and reprimand them. "They called [the disciples], and commanded them not to speak at all nor teach in the name of Jesus" (verse 18).

Immediately Peter and John refused to cooperate. "For we cannot but speak the things which we have seen and heard" (verse 20). They knew it wasn't the end, though. They went to the other apostles and held a prayer meeting, pleading with God to give them boldness to speak the truth. "When they heard that, they lifted up their voice to God with one accord, and said, Lord, thou art God, which hast made heaven, and earth, and the sea, and all that in them is. . . . And now, Lord, behold their threatenings: and grant unto thy servants, that with all boldness they may speak thy word" (verses 24, 29).

Let us be bold in sharing Your truth, Lord.

Stephen Pleads for His Enemies

Lord Jesus, receive my spirit. . . . Lay not this sin to their charge.
Acts 7:59–60

The religious leaders couldn't stand it. The teachings of Christ's disciples were making them angry. They tried to stop them, but the persecution just seemed to spur them into action. Now there was this business of Stephen. He was a good man. He had been chosen by the apostles as one who would care for the widows of the church. He was an honest man; he had a good reputation.

The leaders couldn't stand him, so they conspired to get rid of him. Even at his defense trial, his accusers couldn't escape his testimony. He even went back to Abraham to show the validity of Jesus' claim to be the Messiah; but instead of acknowledging the truth, they dragged Stephen out and began to stone him. As his life faded away, Stephen made two requests: "Lord Jesus, receive my spirit. And he kneeled down, and cried with a loud voice, Lord, lay not this sin to their charge" (Acts 7:59–60).

Then Stephen died, never knowing if his final defense reached anyone. But it did. A man named Saul stood there condoning the stoning, but the Gospel took hold, and he became the apostle Paul.

Allow our testimony to reach someone,
even when we don't know it, Lord.

God Gets Saul's Attention

Lord, what wilt thou have me to do?
ACTS 9:6

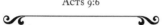

Sometimes when God wants to get our attention, all it takes is a still, small voice. Other times it takes something more dramatic. Think about Jonah for a minute. If getting swallowed by a whale didn't get his attention, is there anything that would have? What about Balaam? It took a conversation with his donkey for God to get ahold of him.

Now here was Saul, a Christ-hating, religious Pharisee. He was on a mission full of hatred. He would have liked nothing more than to obliterate all Christians, but God was stronger. As Saul neared his destination, he was blinded by a bright light and brought to his knees. He was brought to a place where he could no longer run from Jesus. "Saul, Saul, why persecutest thou me? And he said, Who art thou, Lord?" (Acts 9:4–5).

Evidently Saul had been under conviction for a while, because Jesus answered, "I am Jesus whom thou persecutest: it is hard for thee to kick against the pricks" (verse 5).

God had gotten Saul's attention. Saul couldn't run from God any longer. "He trembling and astonished said, Lord, what wilt thou have me to do?" (verse 6).

*Lord, help us listen right away so You don't
have to do something huge to get our attention.*

The Hesitation of Ananias

Lord, I have heard by many of this man, how much evil
he hath done to thy saints at Jerusalem.
Acts 9:13

Ananias was a godly man, evidently in close fellowship with His heavenly Father. When God called out to him, he was immediately eager to hear what God had to say. What God had to say must have shaken him to the core. "Enquire in the house of Judas for one called Saul, of Tarsus: for, behold, he prayeth" (Acts 9:11).

What! Didn't God know about Saul? This same Saul who held the coats of those who stoned Stephen! This was the same man who even now intended to imprison Christ's followers at Damascus. Surely Ananias hadn't heard God correctly! "Lord, I have heard by many of this man, how much evil he hath done to thy saints at Jerusalem: and here he hath authority from the chief priests to bind all that call on thy name" (verses 13–14). Ananias had forgotten that God was seeing the big picture. He was momentarily paralyzed by fear. Then God gently nudged Ananias ahead. Little did Ananias realize that he would bear the Good News to the man who would have such great influence on Christ's kingdom!

O Lord, when we are inclined to fear,
remind us that You already know the outcome.

Cornelius, an Ernest Man's Prayer

What is it, Lord?
ACTS 10:4

God's ways are so perfect that the orchestration of them can only be successful. Consider Cornelius, an important man in his own right. He had power in the Roman army. He was surrounded by family and servants. Yet he knew something was missing.

He was evidently a religious man, for Acts 10:2 tells us that he was "a devout man, and one that feared God with all his house, which gave much alms to the people, and prayed to God always." Still Cornelius was not at peace. He tried so hard to please this God whom he feared, but he didn't understand that it was a relationship with Jesus that he needed.

Day in and day out, he prayed and tried to reach God in his own way. Then in God's perfect time, He sent an angel to Cornelius in a vision. "Thy prayers and thine alms are come up for a memorial before God. And now send men to Joppa, and call for one Simon, whose surname is Peter: . . .he shall tell thee what thou oughtest to do" (Acts 10:4–6).

At last Cornelius would have some answers and peace with God!

*Thank You, God, that You hear us even when
we don't know what to say.*

Peter's Refusal and Obedience

*Not so, Lord; for I have never eaten any thing
that is common or unclean.*
Acts 10:14

∽ ～

Peter was hungry, but it wasn't yet time to eat, so he chose to spend the extra time in prayer. As he was praying, he fell into a trance and saw a sheet coming down from heaven. On this sheet were a variety of animals that were considered unclean. "There came a voice to him, Rise, Peter; kill, and eat" (Acts 10:13).

Was this a test? Did God want to test him to see if he was so hungry he would eat what was unclean? "But Peter said, Not so, Lord; for I have never eaten any thing that is common or unclean" (verse 14).

He had passed the test—or so he thought! "The voice spake unto him again the second time, What God hath cleansed, that call not thou common" (verse 15).

Three times this happened. Peter knew God was trying to tell him something, but what? About that time, Cornelius's servants arrived, looking for him. "While Peter thought on the vision, the Spirit said unto him, Behold, three men seek thee. Arise therefore, and get thee down, and go with them, doubting nothing: for I have sent them" (verses 19–20).

The Gentiles! God was calling him to take the Gospel to the Gentiles.

*Lord, when You call us to a task, please show us
clearly that it is Your will.*

Paul's Claim in the Faith

*In all these things we are more than conquerors
through him that loved us.*
ROMANS 8:37

Oh the evil and heartache of this world! At times it is overbearing. Temptation threatens to overtake. Fear rears its ugly head. Christians are killed or persecuted for their faith. At times like this, it is easy to question the love and presence of God. It is not a situation unique to this day and age, though. The Christians of Paul's day faced similar doubt and questions.

Satan and his demons have been at work for a long time. Their goal is to keep others from coming to Christ. They use many tactics to accomplish this: trials, difficulty, hunger, poverty, danger, and more. If Satan can hold back a believer from sharing Christ or living for the Lord, he will, in part, have accomplished his goal.

Paul exhorts the believer: "For I am persuaded, that neither death, nor life, nor angels, nor principalities, nor powers, nor things present, nor things to come, nor height, nor depth, nor any other creature, shall be able to separate us from the love of God, which is in Christ Jesus our Lord" (Romans 8:38–39).

Yes, Satan throws many fiery darts, but the love of God is stronger.

*Thank You, Lord, that none of the evils of the world
can separate us from Your love.*

Praise of Paul

For of him, and through him, and to him, are all things:
to whom be glory for ever. Amen.
ROMANS 11:36

The greatness of God is overwhelming. His ways are often incomprehensible. He is awesome. He is wise. He is God.

It is often tempting to elevate Paul or the apostles or great heroes of the faith to a status of greatness, but even they fell in humility before almighty God. Paul declared, "O the depth of the riches both of the wisdom and knowledge of God! how unsearchable are his judgments, and his ways past finding out!" (Romans 11:33). He was echoing the mighty men of the past who recognized their frailty before the God of the universe.

Hundreds of years before Paul, David penned similar words: "Thy righteousness is like the great mountains; thy judgments are a great deep: O Lord, thou preservest man and beast" (Psalm 36:6).

We do not always understand God's ways. These are not for us to know. Too often we are full of our own wisdom and a false sense of pride when we should be on our knees before El Elyon—the Most High God. Let us never cease to praise Him!

O God, it is only by You that we have our breath.
May we use it always to offer You praise!

Paul's Encouragement

*Now to him that is of power to stablish you according to my gospel,
and the preaching of Jesus Christ, according to the revelation of
the mystery, which was kept secret since the world began.*
ROMANS 16:25

Shortly before Jesus ascended into heaven, He commanded His disciples, "Go ye into all the world, and preach the Gospel to every creature" (Mark 16:15). On the day of Pentecost, the Holy Spirit filled the disciples, and through God's power they began to share the Gospel in languages they did not know. Many people were saved, and the Gospel was spread to the Gentiles.

At the time that Paul wrote the book of Romans, he had not yet met the believers at Rome. It was a thriving church, however, likely a result of the Christians who were saved on the day of Pentecost and then returned to Rome to share the gift of salvation.

Paul's desire was to encourage these believers, so he wrote them a letter. Throughout the book of Romans, Paul clearly emphasized the freedom we have through salvation and then explained true Christian living.

He concluded his letter joyfully. Even though Christ first revealed salvation to the Jews, it is not only for the Jews! "Now is made manifest, and by the scriptures of the prophets, according to the commandment of the everlasting God, made known to all nations for the obedience of faith" (Romans 16:26).

Thank You, Jesus, for the gift of salvation!

Paul's Reminder to the Galatians

Grace be to you and peace from God the Father,
and from our Lord Jesus Christ.
GALATIANS 1:3

The Galatian church had a big problem, but it wasn't a new problem. It went back to the Garden of Eden where the serpent questioned Eve, saying, "Yea, hath God said. . . ?" (Genesis 3:1).

Satan wants very much for us to question God. At any opportunity, he will cause us to doubt the complete truth of God's Word. He was certainly not happy with how the true Gospel was spreading. He had lost a strong ally in Paul and was determined to work against him, so he gathered a new crowd—the Judaizers.

From the very beginning, Paul had taught salvation by grace through faith alone. Through His death, burial, and resurrection, Christ had already defeated Satan. Satan knew he couldn't blatantly refute that, so he again used subtle methods. He began to whisper in the hearts of certain Jewish Christians, "The blood is not enough. Tell the Gentiles they have to adopt Jewish customs, too." Thus the works of man were added to the already complete Gospel.

Paul was vigilant. He immediately addressed the situation. He reminded them that Christ "gave himself for our sins, that he might deliver us from this present evil world, according to the will of God and our Father" (Galatians 1:4).

Jesus, Your work of salvation is complete. Let us not
be so prideful as to think we can add to it.

Paul's Prayer in Behalf of the Ephesians

*For this cause I bow my knees unto the Father
of our Lord Jesus Christ.*
EPHESIANS 3:14

Paul desired that the Ephesian brethren understand more fully what it was to be a child of God. He made sure they understood that through Christ, all believers are part of the same family: "Of whom the whole family in heaven and earth is named" (Ephesians 3:15).

He prayed that they would be strengthened through the working of the Holy Spirit. He understood the joy of walking with Jesus, but he also recognized that there would be challenges throughout the journey. It was important that the Ephesians knew it wouldn't be in their own strength that they would walk: "That he would grant you, according to the riches of his glory, to be strengthened with might by his Spirit in the inner man" (Ephesians 3:16).

As Paul prayed that the Ephesians would be strengthened through the Holy Spirit, he also prayed that they would understand the love of Christ, "which passeth knowledge, that ye might be filled with all the fulness of God" (verse 19).

After interceding, Paul praised God. "Now unto him that is able to do exceeding abundantly above all that we ask or think, according to the power that worketh in us, unto him be glory in the church by Christ Jesus throughout all ages, world without end. Amen" (verses 20–21).

Heavenly Father, thank You for the work You do in us.

Paul's Prayer for the Colossians

And whatsoever ye do in word or deed, do all in the name of the Lord Jesus, giving thanks to God and the Father by him.
COLOSSIANS 3:17

❧───────────❧

True Christian worship is not passive. It involves action on a regular basis. Paul encouraged the Colossian church to "let the peace of God rule in your hearts, to the which also ye are called in one body; and be ye thankful" (Colossians 3:15).

Satan wants to rob believers of the peace they have in Christ. He casts doubt about our qualification to serve God. He instills fear about the future. He tries to bring up our guilty past. This is nothing new. Paul reminded the Colossians that they had to be actively involved in allowing God's peace to rule in their hearts. They had to choose God's peace over Satan's manipulation.

Another act of worship is to "Let the word of Christ dwell in you richly in all wisdom; teaching and admonishing one another in psalms and hymns and spiritual songs, singing with grace in your hearts to the Lord" (verse 16).

It is possible to worship alone, but what encouragement believers receive when they spend time praising God together! Paul recognized this and reminded the Colossians of it.

Finally, he challenged them, "Whatsoever ye do in word or deed, do all in the name of the Lord Jesus, giving thanks to God and the Father by him" (verse 17).

Lord, we will do all for Your glory!

Paul's Prayer for the Thessalonians

*As ye know how we exhorted and comforted and charged
every one of you, as a father doth his children.*
1 THESSALONIANS 2:11

Paul wanted to visit the church at Thessalonica, but at the time that he wrote his first letter to them, he didn't know if it would happen. Still, he wanted to know how they were doing in their relationship with God, so he sent Timothy to find out.

How pleased Paul was to hear that they continued to walk with God. He reminded them how important it was for them to increase in God's love. "The Lord make you to increase and abound in love one toward another, and toward all men, even as we do toward you. To the end he may stablish your hearts unblameable in holiness before God, even our Father, at the coming of our Lord Jesus Christ with all his saints" (1 Thessalonians 3:12–13).

God is not silent in His word on the role that love plays in the Christian's relationship to Him and to other believers. It is foundational, for if the command to love God and others is fulfilled, all other areas of Christian growth and service will come more readily.

Paul's challenge to the Thessalonians is universal. It is timeless. It is difficult, but the resulting joy is beyond measure.

Father, increase our love for You!

Paul's Prayer for Timothy

Fight the good fight of faith, lay hold on eternal life,
whereunto thou art also called, and hast professed
a good profession before many witnesses.
1 TIMOTHY 6:12

The path before Timothy was one filled with great opportunity. He was a young man, and he still had much of his lifetime to minister for Christ. Paul knew this, and having already experienced much of what Timothy would face, he prayed for his friend and offered him words of advice and encouragement.

Timothy would face temptation as one always does when seeking to serve God. "But thou, O man of God, flee these things; and follow after righteousness, godliness, faith, love, patience, meekness" (1 Timothy 6:11).

As with anyone who truly desires to serve God, Timothy must remain pure before Him. "That thou keep this commandment without spot, unrebukable, until the appearing of our Lord Jesus Christ" (verse 14).

Because he was in a position of influence, Timothy also needed to be an encouragement to other believers: "Laying up in store for themselves a good foundation against the time to come, that they may lay hold on eternal life" (verse 19).

The words Paul wrote to Timothy are for us all. Let us fight the good fight!

Our hearts' desire is that we might have an
impact on others for You, Father.

Prayer for the Hebrews

Now the God of peace, that brought again from the dead
our Lord Jesus, that great shepherd of the sheep, through the blood
of the everlasting covenant, make you perfect in
every good work to do his will.
HEBREWS 13:20–21

God, who is the God of peace, is the only one who is able to give true peace. The author of this letter to the Hebrews understood how much God wanted His people to enjoy this peace, but he knew that the people would have to choose to accept this blessing. "I beseech you, brethren, suffer the word of exhortation: for I have written a letter unto you in few words" (Hebrews 13:22).

The writer was not trying to overwhelm his readers. He simply wanted them to understand that his prayer for them was that they would allow God's peace to be manifested in their lives.

How often do Christians turn away from the peace that is available from our heavenly Father? It might be a passive rejection. We don't intentionally say, "I don't want God's peace. Instead, we just take over. We try to solve things on our own, to do things our way. Before long our relationship with God is shallow at best, and the peace we could have had through Him has turned to turmoil by our own invitation.

Lord, I will accept the peace You offer.
I surrender completely to You.

The Power of Prayer

The effectual fervent prayer of a righteous man availeth much.
JAMES 5:16

For what should we pray? What if God only moved according to how we pray? Would our prayer lives be different?

James, a half brother of Jesus, was one of the early Church leaders. At the time, however, the Church was scattered as a result of religious persecution. James wrote to encourage them as they faced many difficult times. He concluded his letter by challenging them to pray.

Pray for those who are facing trials. Offer prayers of praise with those who are rejoicing. Pray for the sick and dying. Share your weaknesses with other Christians that they might bring your name before the throne of grace. Perhaps these all sound like "typical" prayers, but James didn't stop here. "Elias was a man subject to like passions as we are, and he prayed earnestly that it might not rain: and it rained not on the earth by the space of three years and six months" (James 5:17).

Elias was just like anyone else, but he took prayer seriously. He prayed for something rather unconventional, and God answered his prayer in a big way. He knew there was nothing too big or too small to bring before God.

God wants us to bring our requests to Him. He wants us to offer Him praise. He wants us to truly get ahold of Him.

Thank You, Father, for answered prayer.

John's Prayer for Children

I have no greater joy than to hear that my
children walk in truth.
3 John 1:4

John's heart was full of joy as he wrote to his beloved "children"—those whom he had led to Christ. As parents rejoice when their children are living right, so John rejoiced that his "children" were walking in the truth. "For I rejoiced greatly, when the brethren came and testified of the truth that is in thee, even as thou walkest in the truth" (3 John 1:3).

Often parents-to-be are asked if they are hoping for a boy or a girl, and many times they will reply that really they are just praying for a healthy baby. John takes that a step further as he prays for his spiritual children. "Beloved, I wish above all things that thou mayest prosper and be in health, even as thy soul prospereth" (verse 2).

John knew that these believers were enjoying spiritual health. They had a testimony of walking in the truth, and his prayer was that because they were spiritually right that God would physically bless them as well.

Too many times parents get this backward and are more concerned with temporal blessings. While it is right to pray for our physical and earthly needs, it is the condition of the soul that matters most. Let's put the eternal first.

Lord, as our children serve You, please bless their lives.

Prayer to Keep Believers from Stumbling

Now unto him that is able to keep you from falling,
and to present you faultless before the presence
of his glory with exceeding joy.
JUDE 1:24

What is the purpose of a flashlight? It is to cast just enough light to keep a person from stumbling in the darkness. It is enough light to show you the way you need to go without revealing everything that is around you. There are times that if we could see more, we would become overwhelmed by the sheer amount of work that needed to be done, and any thought of rest would be gone.

We live in a world that is darkened by sin. There are plenty of opportunities for us to falter. Christ even told Simon Peter that Satan wanted to have him. "But I have prayed for thee, that thy faith fail not" (Luke 22:32).

Satan will tempt us. Trials will come our way. The path in front of us will be difficult at times, but it is Christ who can keep us from falling, and it is He who deserves the praise as we successfully navigate our Christian walk. "Now unto him that is able to keep you from falling, and to present you faultless before the presence of his glory with exceeding joy, to the only wise God our Saviour, be glory and majesty, dominion and power, both now and ever. Amen" (Jude 1:24–25).

Please keep us safe on the journey of life, dear Jesus.

John's Prayer for the Seven Churches of Asia

*And from Jesus Christ, who is the faithful witness,
and the first begotten of the dead, and the prince
of the kings of the earth.*
REVELATION 1:5

While Christ walked this earth, John was one of His closest friends. John was one of the first to leave his job and follow Jesus. At the Last Supper, he sat next to Jesus and quietly said, "Who is it?" when Jesus said that one of His own would betray Him. He witnessed the crucifixion and saw the empty tomb and risen Savior, and John continued to serve Him after Christ ascended to heaven.

Now, because of his work for Christ, John found himself exiled to the desolate island of Patmos. Even from there he continued to encourage fellow believers. As he wrote to the seven churches at Asia, he reminded them that it isn't their work, but the work of the risen Christ that saved them: "From Jesus Christ, who is the faithful witness, and the first begotten of the dead, and the prince of the kings of the earth. Unto him that loved us, and washed us from our sins in his own blood, and hath made us kings and priests unto God and his Father; to him be glory and dominion for ever and ever. Amen" (Revelation 1:5–6).

*Thank You, Lord, that we can serve You because
of Your complete work of salvation.*

Creatures Worship God

Holy, holy, holy, Lord God Almighty.
REVELATION 4:8

Heaven will be filled with the worship of God! John was given just a glimpse of this in his vision as he saw the variety of creatures and people who worshipped day and night.

The things that he saw were like none other he had ever seen, but the worship of God Almighty stood out to Him. First he noticed the creatures: "The four beasts had each of them six wings about him; and they were full of eyes within: and they rest not day and night, saying, Holy, holy, holy, Lord God Almighty, which was, and is, and is to come" (Revelation 4:8). These creatures, strange as they were, could not keep from praising God. As the twenty-four elders around the throne witnessed this, they too were compelled to worship Christ.

How often does God's creation prompt us to praise God? Consider the intricacy of a tiny yet beautifully amazing hummingbird or the majestic sight of an autumn sunrise. We must agree with the psalmist when he says, "The heavens declare the glory of God; and the firmament sheweth his handywork" (Psalm 19:1).

When we witness such majesty, we too should be prompted to deeper worship of our great God.

O God, You are God Almighty, and we will praise You!

Elders Worship God

Thou art worthy, O Lord,
to receive glory and honour and power.
REVELATION 4:11

As the twenty-four elders around God's throne observed the unusual creatures who were worshipping God, they were reminded of a couple things. First, they acknowledged that God is worthy of all glory and praise offered to him. Second, they were reminded that God's purpose in creating them and everything else was ultimately to offer Him praise. "Thou art worthy, O Lord, to receive glory and honour and power: for thou hast created all things, and for thy pleasure they are and were created" (Revelation 4:11).

The questions we must all ask ourselves are these: "Am I fulfilling God's purpose for creating me? How can I better bring glory to God?" We live in a world that, in general, has forgotten this. We have bought into Satan's lie that says we are here to please ourselves, and we have "changed the truth of God into a lie, and worshipped and served the creature more than the Creator, who is blessed for ever. Amen" (Romans 1:25).

It is time we repent and turn our attention to the Lord, who is worthy of our praise.

God, we worship You, and You alone.

New Song of the Elders

Thou art worthy to take the book,
and to open the seals thereof.
Revelation 5:9

When a person accepts Christ as Savior, he or she is stamped with a seal of Christ's ownership. As a result, only Jesus can open that seal and redeem that soul. As John's vision continued, he saw a book that was sealed with seven seals. He saw a strong angel who was unable to open the seals. The angel cried, "Who is worthy to open the book, and to loose the seals thereof?" (Revelation 5:2).

John began to weep as he realized there was none worthy, but one of the elders who was worshipping at the throne told him all was not hopeless. "Weep not: behold, the Lion of the tribe of Judah, the Root of David, hath prevailed to open the book, and to loose the seven seals thereof" (verse 5).

At that moment, John saw a lamb that had been slain. The Lamb stepped forward and a new song began: "Thou art worthy to take the book, and to open the seals thereof: for thou wast slain, and hast redeemed us to God by thy blood out of every kindred, and tongue, and people, and nation; and hast made us unto our God kings and priests: and we shall reign on the earth" (verses 9–10).

Praise You, Jesus! Our names are in Your book,
and we look forward to the day You open it!

Praise of Angels

And I beheld, and I heard the voice of many angels round
about the throne and the beasts and the elders:
and the number of them was ten thousand times
ten thousand, and thousands of thousands.
REVELATION 5:11

Have you ever had the opportunity to hear a really large choir or even a smaller choir in a building with good acoustics? Try to recall how majestic it sounded. Now turn your thoughts to heaven and imagine if you can the scene being played out before John.

He had gone from a state of hopelessness, believing no one was worthy to open the sealed book, to joy as the elders begin to praise the Lamb. Now he could only stand in awe as the voices of tens of thousands joined together to lift up praise to the Lamb. "Worthy is the Lamb that was slain to receive power, and riches, and wisdom, and strength, and honour, and glory, and blessing" (Revelation 5:12).

These angels and beasts had not needed to experience the redemption of Christ, yet they were still overwhelmed by His greatness. They realized that He alone was worthy of all the adulation they were putting on Him. As Christians, we know we have been redeemed, but too often we fail to offer the praise that Christ deserves. What a day it will be when we can praise Him face-to-face!

Heavenly Father, we can't praise You enough
for Your amazing work of salvation!

Every Knee Shall Bow

Blessing, and honour, and glory, and power,
be unto him that sitteth upon the throne.
REVELATION 5:13

There is coming a day when all creation will bow in worship to the King of kings—the creator of the universe. They won't be able to help it. "Every creature which is in heaven, and on the earth, and under the earth, and such as are in the sea, and all that are in them, heard I saying, Blessing, and honour, and glory, and power, be unto him that sitteth upon the throne, and unto the Lamb for ever and ever" (Revelation 5:13).

The opening of this book is of great importance to all of creation, and this is evidenced when all raise their voice as one in praise to Him who is found worthy to open it. What made Him worthy? His perfect blood spilled out to cover a multitude of sins. There was no other way for mankind to receive salvation.

All creation will one day realize this and fall before God, but for many it will be too late. Oh that all would receive the gift of the Lamb, that their worship would be in joy and not fear. "Behold, now is the accepted time; behold, now is the day of salvation" (2 Corinthians 6:2).

We pray that those who have not yet come to You,
Jesus, will accept You today!

The Prayer of the Martyrs

How long, O Lord, holy and true,
dost thou not judge and avenge our blood?
REVELATION 6:10

In the 1500s a man named John Foxe fled the persecution of Queen Mary, who was torturing those who held Reformed views. While in hiding, he put together a collection of stories of those who had been martyred for their faith. We know this collection as *Foxe's Book of Martyrs*. It takes time to read it, but it is by no means a complete list of martyrs, even for that time—and that was five hundred years ago!

Persecution and killing of the saints is no surprise to God. It began before Jesus walked the earth. It happened to His apostles. Imagine John as he sees this fifth seal opened. "They cried with a loud voice, saying, How long, O Lord, holy and true, dost thou not judge and avenge our blood on them that dwell on the earth?" (Revelation 6:10). Did John see his brother, his fellow apostles who had died for their faith, as they cried out before God?

Persecution of Christians is real today, but there is coming a day when these saints and their persecutors will receive their just reward.

Lord, we ask that You would strengthen those
being tortured for their faith.

Complete Praise and Worship

*And all the angels stood round about the throne,
and about the elders and the four beasts, and fell before
the throne on their faces, and worshipped God.*
REVELATION 7:11

As Christians we talk often about how praise and worship of God should be part of our lives. We memorize verses, such as 1 Thessalonians 5:18, and we do our best to offer our praise to God.

A day is coming when we will stand in the presence of almighty God and will be part of a worship service that our imperfect minds can only begin to grasp. We thank God now for our salvation, but when we stand before Him face-to-face, we will raise our voices more loudly than ever and cry, "Salvation to our God which sitteth upon the throne, and unto the Lamb" (Revelation 7:10).

As we are worshipping, the angels, the elders, and the four living creatures will again be compelled to join in the mighty chorus. "Saying, Amen: Blessing, and glory, and wisdom, and thanksgiving, and honour, and power, and might, be unto our God for ever and ever. Amen" (verse 12).

Let us take every opportunity we have now to praise God as we await this coming day of perfect worship. "By him therefore let us offer the sacrifice of praise to God continually, that is, the fruit of our lips giving thanks to his name" (Hebrews 13:15).

God, You alone are worthy of our praise!

A Marriage to Praise

*He saith unto me, Write, Blessed are they which are called
unto the marriage supper of the Lamb. And he saith
unto me, These are the true sayings of God.*
REVELATION 19:9

As John's vision continued, a great celebration was beginning—
the marriage supper of Christ, the Lamb. Prior to the celebration,
the praise had already started. "After these things I heard a great
voice of much people in heaven, saying, Alleluia, Salvation, and
glory, and honour, and power, unto the Lord our God" (Revelation 19:1).

After all, there is much for which to praise Jesus. As Revelation
19:2 continues, Jesus has brought judgment on the corrupt leaders
of the earth who for so long deceived mankind and tortured the
servants of Christ. Now the great whore had been destroyed.
"Again they said, Alleluia. And her smoke rose up for ever and
ever" (verse 3).

The rejoicing continued, and John described the sound as "the
voice of a great multitude, and as the voice of many waters, and as
the voice of mighty thunderings, saying, Alleluia: for the Lord God
omnipotent reigneth" (verse 6).

Then came the moment for which Christ's bride had waited
for centuries. "Let us be glad and rejoice, and give honour to him:
for the marriage of the Lamb is come, and his wife hath made
herself ready" (verse 7).

Thank You, God, for giving us hope in our future.

Prayers for Christ's Return

Even so, come, Lord Jesus.
REVELATION 22:20

The apostles had been looking for the second coming of Christ from the time He returned to heaven. Jesus had promised that He would come for them, and they were eager for this event (John 14:3). Immediately following Jesus' ascension, two angels came to them and said, "Ye men of Galilee, why stand ye gazing up into heaven? this same Jesus, which is taken up from you into heaven, shall so come in like manner as ye have seen him go into heaven" (Acts 1:11).

The apostles began immediately looking for Jesus to return, and they believed it would be during their lifetime. When it didn't happen as expected, Peter reminded the early Christians that "the Lord is not slack concerning his promise, as some men count slackness; but is longsuffering to us-ward, not willing that any should perish, but that all should come to repentance" (2 Peter 3:9).

Then, as John experienced His vision, he was again reminded of the coming of Christ. "He which testifieth these things saith, Surely I come quickly." John, who had been waiting many years for this, replied, "Even so, come, Lord Jesus" (Revelation 22:20).

Dear Jesus, we are looking forward to Your return.
With John, we plead, come quickly.

Scripture Index

OLD TESTAMENT

NEW TESTAMENT

Read Through the Bible in a Year